ARCHITECTURAL
GRAPHICS
AND
COMMUNICATION

ARCHITECTURAL GRAPHICS AND COMMUNICATION

Third Edition

KENDALL/HUNT PUBLISHING COMPANY
4050 Westmark Drive   Dubuque, Iowa 52002

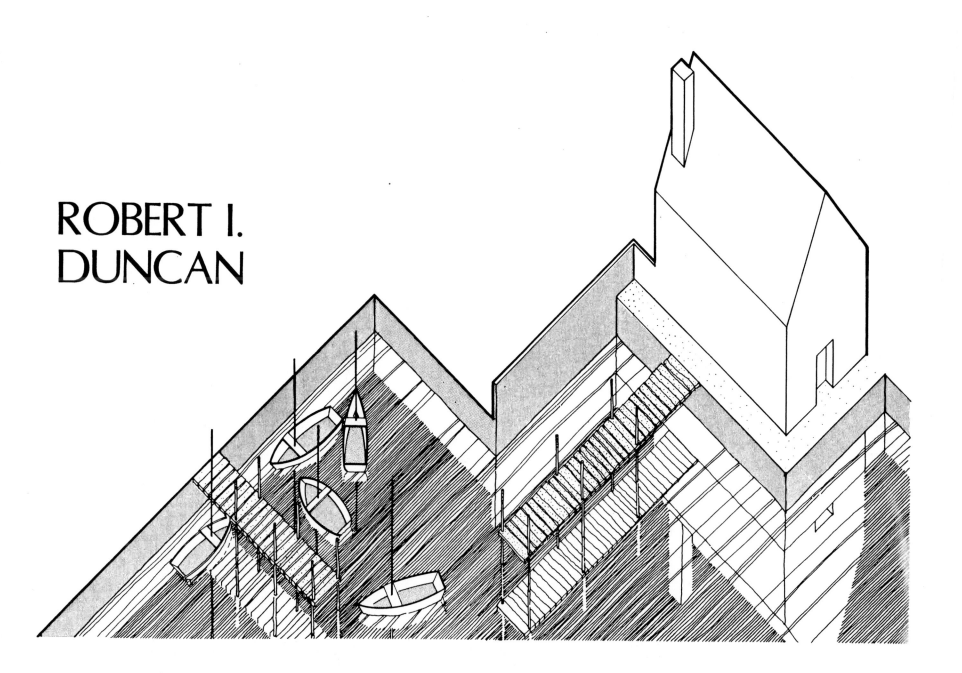

ROBERT I.
DUNCAN

This book is dedicated to
Randy and Heather
Duncan

CONTENTS

PREFACE

This text is intended for beginning students in architecture and interior design. Its emphasis is on basic architectural graphics with an introduction to lettering, use of instruments and essential methods of orthographic drawing and projection. Also included are methods for visual thinking and analysis in both two and three dimensions presented through numerous illustrations and examples. When used in conjunction with the problems book, *Architectural Graphics and Communication Problems,* the text provides a reference for the study of architectural graphic problem solving techniques and procedures. Other important topics related to architectural graphics which are included are presentation drawings, diagramming, and methods of drawing which are considered prerequisites to architectural and interior design. A major objective of the text is to provide the beginning student with the necessary information to communicate design ideas in a logical and acceptable manner suitable for the architectural profession.

It should be noted that the numerous graphical techniques presented in this book are intended to provide the student with an introduction to appropriate methods of architectural representation. Since architectural graphics plays a strong role in the design process, the information and techniques developed in this text are intended to help the beginning student express and communicate basic ideas while exploring the larger problem of architectural design. As such, a major emphasis of this text is to provide a variety of methods for visual thinking, expression and communication.

An important feature of this textbook are the review questions and problems located in the back of the book. These questions are intended to highlight important points of each chapter and are to be used as a method of review and questioning. They can be assigned as a regular part of the course or used when necessary.

Robert I. Duncan
Lincoln, Nebraska

ACKNOWLEDGMENTS

The original text was published in 1980 with a number of key individuals assisting in the preparation of the book. Numerous professionals and their associates contributed important drawings for the chapters on presentation drawings and diagramming. Faculty and administration at the University of Nebraska also provided their support and encouragement. The second edition and now the third edition also has its cast of supporting players. Many helpful ideas from interested individuals from a wide variety of schools and universities associated with architectural graphics and its instruction have provided their ideas and suggestions regarding material presented in the text. This particular edition has been revised and updated to meet new needs. It is anticipated that such attention will result in a text which is more meaningful and instructional for both the teacher and the student. This text is a product of instructor/student input and an expression of thanks is conveyed to all who have offered their ideas.

ARCHITECTURAL
GRAPHICS
AND
COMMUNICATION

CHAPTER 1

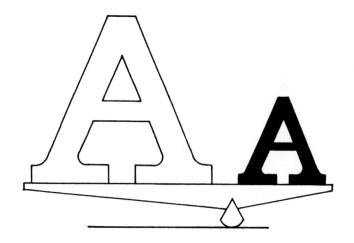

LETTERING

LETTERING AS A COMPOSITIONAL ELEMENT

All lettering and graphic symbols are considered as elements which must relate in the total composition of a architectural presentation. Their impact on the effect of the composition is based upon several important relationships. One such relationship is that of achieving balance. Balance is an optical condition in which several devices are used to create the experience of resolution within a composition. This is done by:

SIZE: 1. In a presentation, size should be determined by ''readability'' from the distance intended.
2. Maintaining good proportions between the letters or graphic symbols with relation to the overall drawing size. This often means considering figure-ground relationships so that the observer is not mislead with respect to minor information.

WEIGHT: Refers to the visual weight as opposed to physical weight. Often a large letter with bold lines will be required for ''readability'' from certain distances, but a lighter value is required to maintain a balanced composition. Thus some letters or symbols may be outlined to reduce their weight.

LOCATION: The placement of lettering or graphic symbols are located to achieve an overall organization to the scheme. Some placement is dictated by convention and practice, such as title strips, scale, etc.

ABCDEFGHIJKLMNOPQRST

ABCDEF 123456

ABCDEFGH

ABCD

SIZE

WEIGHT

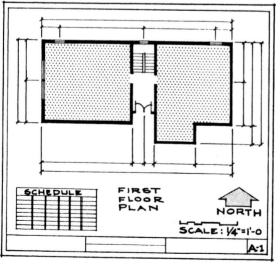

LOCATION

Good lettering is a basic requirement for those concerned with architecture and related sciences. This is very true if the individual is dependent upon free-hand lettering as a method of communication. Generally, everyone will develop their own style of lettering and its character will depend upon the individual's assessment of suitability. Some individuals are more comfortable with a very basic standard lettering style, whereas others are not satisfied unless the letters reflect some of their own individual character. Regardless of the style used, there are several important principles to consider when doing any lettering activity.

GUIDELINES: Are a must item if consistency and uniformity are important. They are placed on the drawing very lightly and allowed to remain. Usually if a duplicate print is made they will not reproduce.

PROPORTION: Proportion is the relationship of height to width, not mathematical but a matter of good judgement.

ABCDIQR HLETJ DPELHRTNX
JUST RIGHT   → TOO WIDE   → ← TOO NARROW

SPACING: Spacing is based upon what is considered legible and pleasing to the eye. This relates to:
   1. Spacing of individual letters within the words of a sentence. This is achieved by keeping the net area between letters equal as opposed to keeping the distances exact.

TECHNIQUE OF LETTERING

   2. Spacing of individual words within a sentence for readibility. A simple rule to follow is to keep the space between words at least equal to or slightly less than the height of the letters being used. One will soon learn to space words by eye rather than by measuring with a scale.

EACH LETTER IS A UNIT OF DESIGN
SPACE EQUALS HEIGHT

CONSISTENCY: This principle will provide the uniformity necessary to achieve desirable lettering skills. The following guides are suggested to help maintain good consistency.

1. Don't combine alphabets. Whatever your lettering style, be consistent in its usage and don't confuse the reader by changing alphabets.
2. Be consistent in use of capital and lower case letters. Don't combine unnecessarily.
3. Keep vertical letters vertical and slanted letters in the proper direction at all times.
4. Pay attention to serifs, if used on certain letters they should be used on all letters.

ABCDEFGHIJKLMNOPQRSTUVWXYZ
abcdefghijklmnopqrstuvwxyz
1234567890 OR 1234567890 OR 1234567890

The lettering guide is an instrument used as an aid when drawing guide lines. It provides for a uniform spacing between lines and ensures consistency in the heights of letters. The circular dial on the guide is rotated until the proper number for the height of letter desired is opposite the mark on the lower part of the guide. This mark represents the understood denominator of a fraction which is 32. Thus placing the dial with the number 8 on the mark will create a fraction 8/32. When reduced, this gives guide lines which are ¼″ in height. The placement of the center guide line is determined by the selection of the first, second, or third row of holes on the guide.

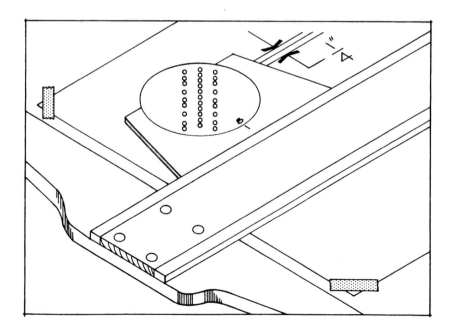

CHAPTER 2

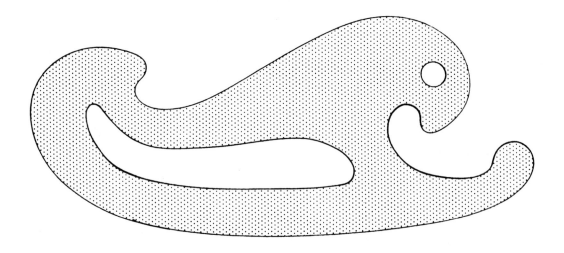

BASIC DRAWING EQUIPMENT

Drawing Pencils

A variety of drafting equipment and supplies are available for the student to choose, and often one may have difficulty in selecting the most appropriate items when such a large number exists. As a rule, one should purchase that equipment which is essential and only add as the situation demands. The items presented in this chapter are considered vital for most types of drafting activity.

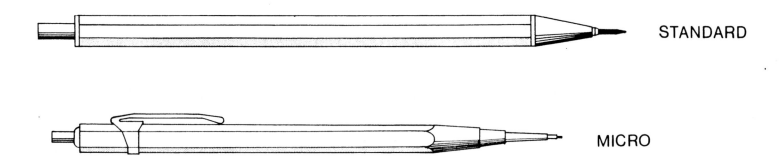

STANDARD

MICRO

Mechanical pencils with individual leads are very popular because the leadholder is designed to fit in the hand and reduce drafting fatigue. This style of leadholder allows for rapid change of leads and sharpening. The two kinds of leadholders illustrated are the standard and the micro. Due to the smallness of the micro lead it does not require sharpening if the holder is rotated sufficiently while drawing. The rotation of the holder ensures that the point remains conical and uniform, thus all lines will be consistent.

WOODEN

The wooden pencil comes in a variety of leads for drawing lines of different weights and intensities. To sharpen, the wood is either sharpened mechanically or cut back with a blade to expose the lead and then pointed by hand on a sandpaper block or with a mechanical pencil pointer.

DRAWING LEADS

When Selecting the proper lead or pencil for a particular drafting activity, a good general rule to follow is: **Use the grade of pencil that will give the type of line suited to the job at hand.** "Suited to the job at hand" means one which will give the intensity of line desired without requiring undue pressure or injury to the surface of the paper. Leads are graded according to degree of hardness ranging from 9H which is very hard to 6B which is very soft. Of the seventeen different grades of leads available, only a few are used for precision drafting. The remaining are either too hard or too soft and are used for other purposes such as freehand drawing and sketching. The following gradations vary with different manufacturers as well as the type of paper used and weather conditions.

9H 8H 7H 6H 5H 4H	Very Hard	This group is used for precision layouts, guide lines, construction lines, and is not recommended for finished drawings as the lines produced are light and thin. Because the leads are so hard it is possible to obtain very accurate drawings using this group.
3H 2H	Medium Hard	This group is the hardest lead suggested for darkening a finished drawing. The 2H lead is very popular because it produces a dark sharp line with a minimum of sharpening.
H F HB	Medium Soft	This group is used for general-purpose work, for technical sketching, for architectural line drawings, for lettering, arrowheads, and for some freehand work.
B 2B 3B 4B 5B 6B	Very Soft	This group is used for freehand work of various kinds. It is almost impossible to keep a sharp conical point on these pencils and leads. They are excellent for presentation drawings where different values of black and gray are desirable.

LEAD POINTERS

Pencils or leads should be sharpened so that a long conical point is obtained. This can be done with a mechanical lead pointer, fine file, or sandpaper pad. Whatever the method of sharpening, the end result should produce a tapered point about ½″ long. The point should be resharpened periodically to ensure maintaining the proper amount of taper. This will help to keep linework uniform and consistent.

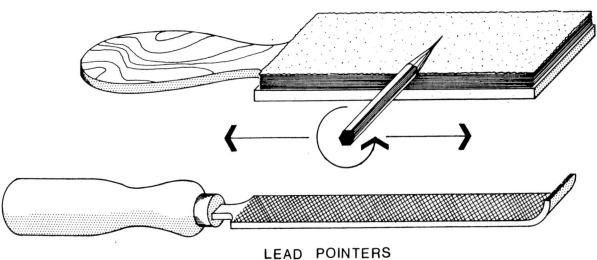

LEAD POINTERS

EERASING SHIELD-DRAFTING BRUSH

The erasing shield is used to remove segments of lines which are in a congested area. As shown, the instrument has many different shaped openings which allow for erasing without disturbing other lines. Simply place the shield over that part of the line to be removed and using a soft eraser scrub away that which is no longer needed. The shield has enough different openings to allow for any configuration. It is also very helpful for protecting the paper while using an electric eraser.

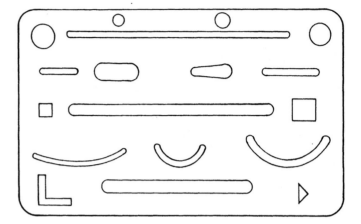

The drafting brush is suggested for brushing away all used eraser particles and helps to keep the drawing surface clean. If too many pieces of eraser dust and particles are left on the drawing surface, they tend to clog the drafting area and cause the pencil to skip reducing the quality of the drawing.

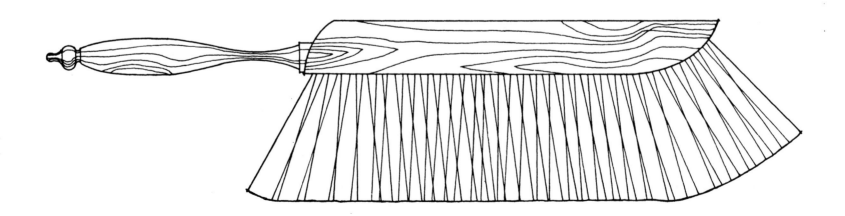

T-Square and Triangles

The T-square, available in a variety of sizes, is used for drawing parallel lines across the paper. It is also used as a rest for the triangles when drawing vertical and inclined lines. When using the T-square, draw lines from left to right across the paper and rotate the pencil slowly so that the point will remain uniform and produce a thin even line. If the line needs to be darker, repeat the operation but never go back and forth over lines, as this will cause the lines to appear as double images.

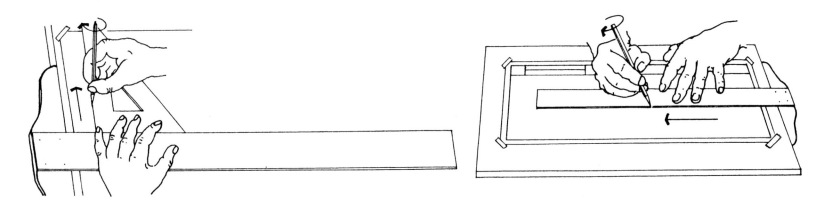

Triangles are also available in a variety of sizes and combinations of 45° and 30°–60°. When used together they can produce a wide number of angles. The adjustable triangle, which has one moveable leg, is very useful for drawing inclined lines and the thumbscrew allows for easy pickup when moving.

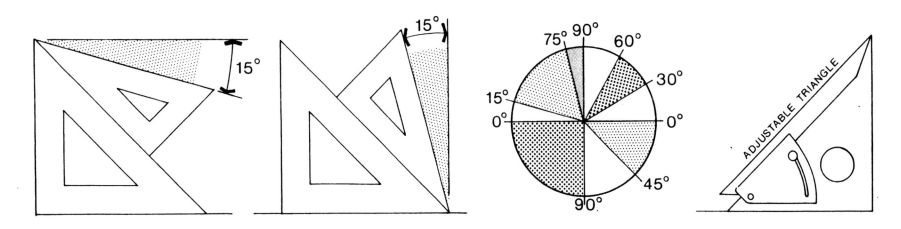

SCALES

Scales are used to draw the building and its components because buildings cannot be practicably drawn full size. The selection of a scale allows for drawings smaller or larger than actual size without making computations. There are numerous types available, but the architect's and the engineer's scales are the most common for architectural use.

ARCHITECT'S SCALE: This scale measures feet, inches, and fractions of inches. Depending upon the type, there is the beveled with 8 scales or the triangular with 11 scales. Scale notations are as follows: 1/16″ = 1′-0, 1/8″ or 1/4″= 1′-0, 3/16″ or 3/32″ = 1′-0, 3/8″ or 3/4″ = 1′-0, 1/2″ or 1″ = 1′-0, 1 1/2″ or 3″ = 1′-0.

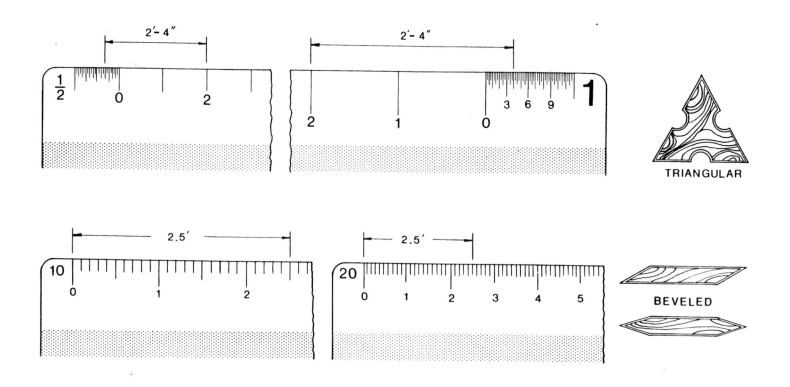

ENGINEER'S SCALE: This scale is used in many branches of engineering and its measurements are based upon the decimal system. The divisions vary from 10 units to an inch up to 60 units to an inch. It is used on such drawings as the site and plot plans. Scale notations are as follows: 1″ = 1′, 1″ = 10′, 1″ = 100′ etc.

METRIC SCALES

The trend towards a metric change from the standard foot/inch system is becoming a reality in the United States and Great Britain. This change has introduced a range of new scales with ratios similar to but slightly different than the standard foot/inch system. The greatest advantage of the metric system is reflected in the ease in which it can be used. The decimal subdivision of the scale 1:1 and 1:100 allows for most drawings to be done with one metric scale. With practice, conversion to metric can be accomplished without too many difficulties, especially since 1 metre(m) = 100 centimetres (cm) = 1000 millimetres(mm). The process of change from feet/inches to metric will appear in the following dimensions: 1/8″=3.17mm, 1/4″=6.35mm, and 1″=25.4mm. In the translation some of these dimensions will be rounded off and will appear as: 1/8″= 3.2mm, 1/4″=6.4mm, and 1″=25mm. Thus the fractional values indicated will hardly be noticeable in scale drawings since they are of minute thickness, but cumulatively they cannot be ignored. The value of one millimetre is approximately that of a pencil line but in fact equals 1.6mm. Therefore it becomes important when detailing conditions that require joining and fitting. The table below illustrates equivalent metric sizes for comparison purposes.

Inches	Millimetres (Exact)
1/16″	1.6mm
1/8″	3.2mm
3/16″	4.8mm
1/4″	6.4mm
5/16″	7.9mm
3/8″	9.5mm
1/2″	12.7mm

The scales shown below give a direct comparison of feet/inches vs metric. When choosing a metric scale, the preferred scale commonly used for different types of drawings is suggested in the chart.

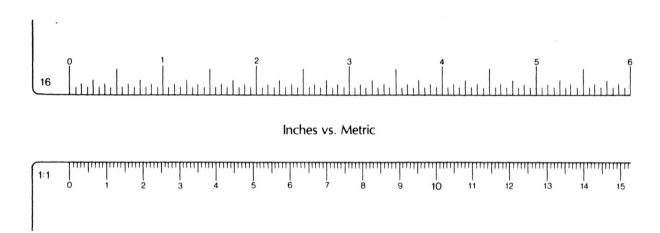

Inches vs. Metric

Type of Drawing	Metric Scale	Foot/Inch Scale
Site Plan	1:500	
	1:200	1/16″ = 1′-0″
Plans/Elevations	1:100	1/8″ = 1′-0″
	1:50	1/4″ = 1′-0″
	1:20	1/2″ = 1′-0″
Sections	1:10	1″ = 1′-0″
Details	1:5	3″ = 1′-0″
	1:1	1″ = 1″

The next three pages illustrate various types of drawings and the metric scales most suitable to use. The site plan shown below was drawn using the metric scale 1:500.

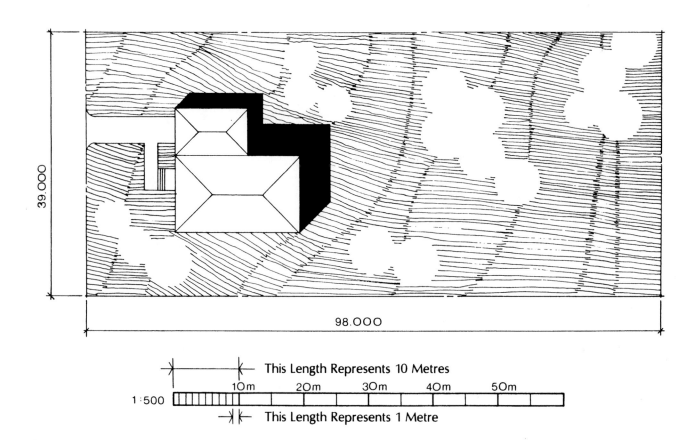

39.000

98.000

This Length Represents 10 Metres

1:500   10m   20m   30m   40m   50m

This Length Represents 1 Metre

Shown below is an example of a floor plan for a house drawn using the metric scale 1:100.

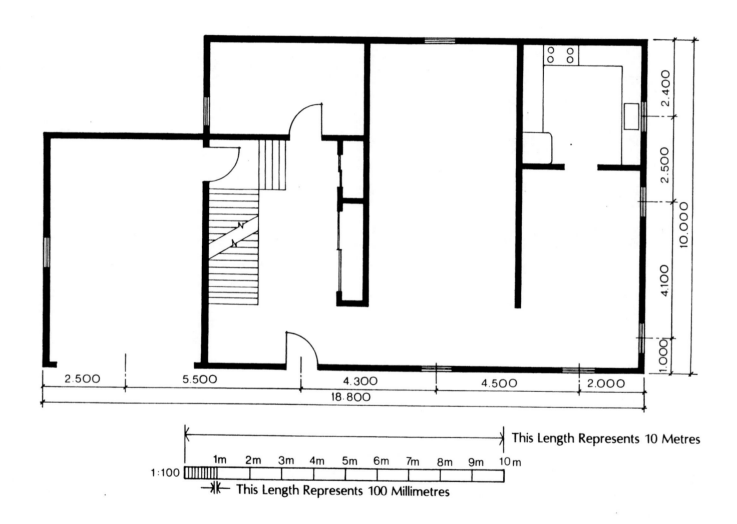

This Length Represents 10 Metres

1:100   1m 2m 3m 4m 5m 6m 7m 8m 9m 10m

This Length Represents 100 Millimetres

The sliding door detail was drawn using the metric scale 1:5.

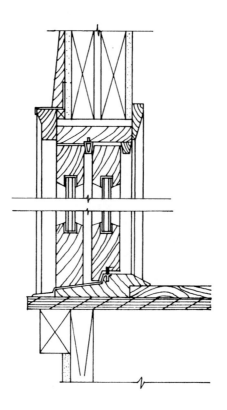

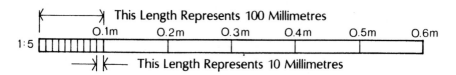

This Length Represents 100 Millimetres

0.1m   0.2m   0.3m   0.4m   0.5m   0.6m

1:5

This Length Represents 10 Millimetres

FRENCH CURVE-TEMPLATES

The French curve is used as a guide when drawing curved lines other than circles or arcs of circles. A wide variety of sizes and shapes are available for purchase. Most curves are made from a rigid plastic, while some others are flexible and will retain the shape into which they are bent. To use the curve, place it in line with a minimum of three points on the curve and draw between any two points. Continue this method until the curve is completed paying attention to the direction of the curve so that it remains smooth and transitional.

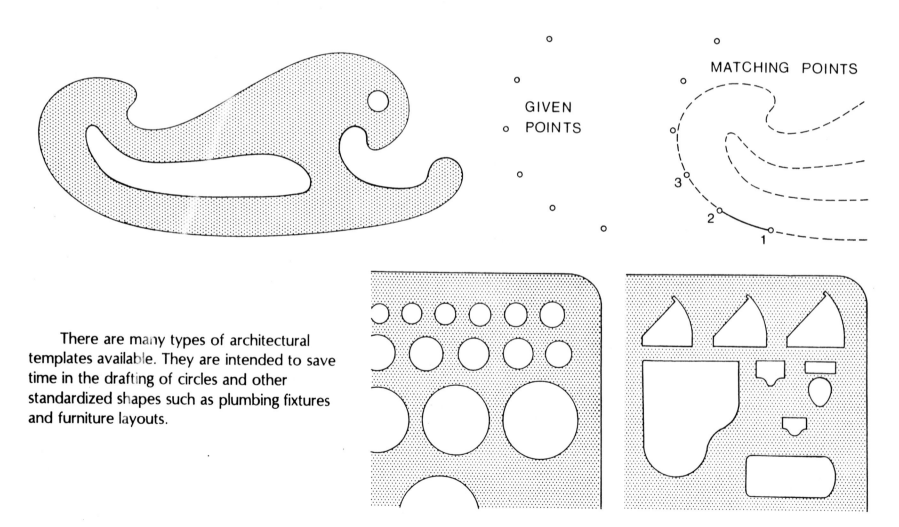

GIVEN POINTS

MATCHING POINTS

There are many types of architectural templates available. They are intended to save time in the drafting of circles and other standardized shapes such as plumbing fixtures and furniture layouts.

COMPASS AND DIVIDERS

There are a wide assortment of drawing instrument sets available for the student to choose. Generally, most sets contain the following: a compass with ruling pen attachment, divider for dividing lines and transferring distances, plus a small number of accessories. Whatever set is selected, the compass will probably be the most used instrument and should receive careful consideration before buying. The bow compass, with its center adjusting screw is recommended for architectural work. When using any compass, remember to use the proper lead for the line weight desired. Also, sharpen the lead point on a sandpaper or file so that it is beveled; this will ensure good sharp lines and uniformity.

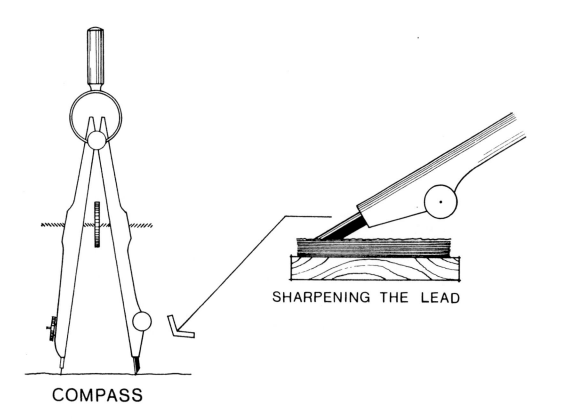

SHARPENING THE LEAD

COMPASS

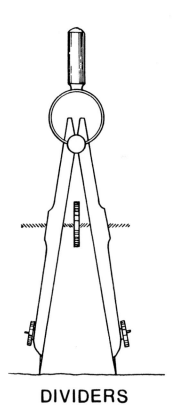

DIVIDERS

QUICK ACTION COMPASS AND DIVIDERS

The "Quick Action" compass has a synchronized precision "scissor-action" thread system which allows the legs to be moved to a desired radius in one quick motion. Unlike the standard bow compass, the compass legs of the "Quick Action" compass can be opened or closed without the need to turn the center wheel. This allows the user to quickly spread the legs of the instrument to the desired approximate position and then fine tune to the exact radius by using the center adjustment wheel. When using a standard six inch compass, circles up to 14" in diameter can be drawn and when used with a beam compass extension the instrument is capable of drawing large circles up to 24" in diameter.

Dividers associated with this style of compass are also "Quick Acting" since they do not have a thread system for spreading the legs. The friction head system used in the instrument ensures smooth operation and pin point accuracy once the legs have been opened and set to the desired position.

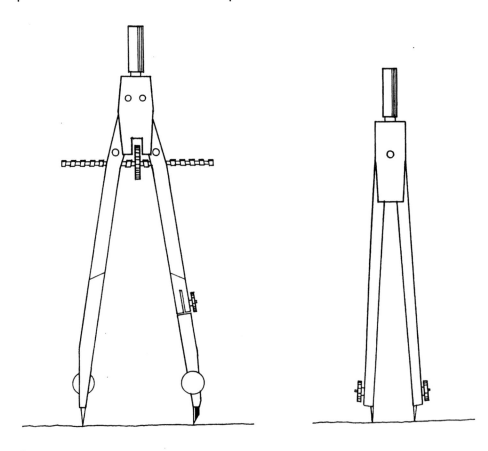

TECHNICAL DRAWING PENS

The technical drawing pen is used for inking on a drawing. Several of its advantages are listed below:

1. It is capable of being used for both freehand and instrument drawing.
2. There are a number of pen points available for different width lines.
3. All of the lines drawn with the pen will be uniform due to point consistency.
4. Straight, curved, or irregular lines can be drawn with the pen either on its own or with attachments.

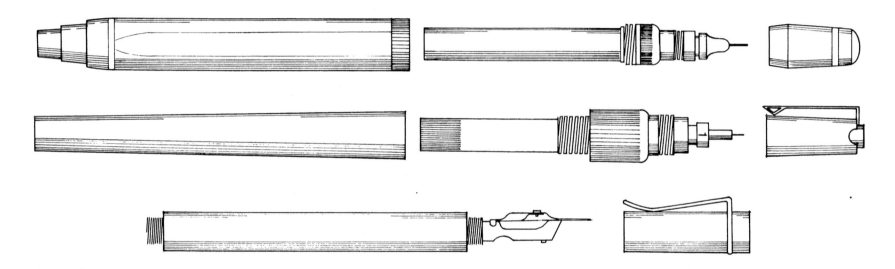

Use a nonclogging waterproof drawing ink which has been specially developed for use in technical pens.

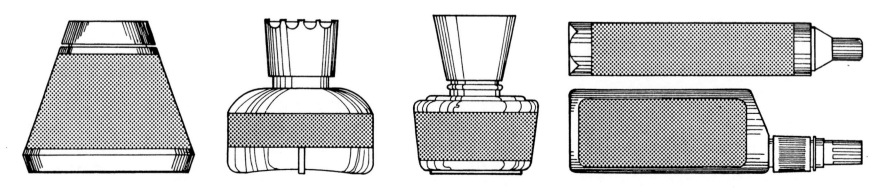

LINE WEIGHTS AND TYPES

In the interest of making drawings easier to read and understand, it is important to use the proper type of line when making a drawing. In addition to the type of line, correct relative line weight should be used. This refers to the thickness or "heaviness" of the line. The actual widths of lines are not as critical as their relative contrast and consistency. The type of line that is used in the communication of architectural data is determined by conventional standards in the profession. When studying the lines below, pay attention to the pattern as well as the weight and thickness.

1. Border Lines

2. Cutting Plane Lines

3. Outline

4. Hidden Lines

5. Break Lines

6. Dimension and Extension Lines

$3'-8$

7. Property Lines

8. Center Lines

9. Section Lines

10. Projection and Construction Lines

GEOMETRIC CONSTRUCTIONS

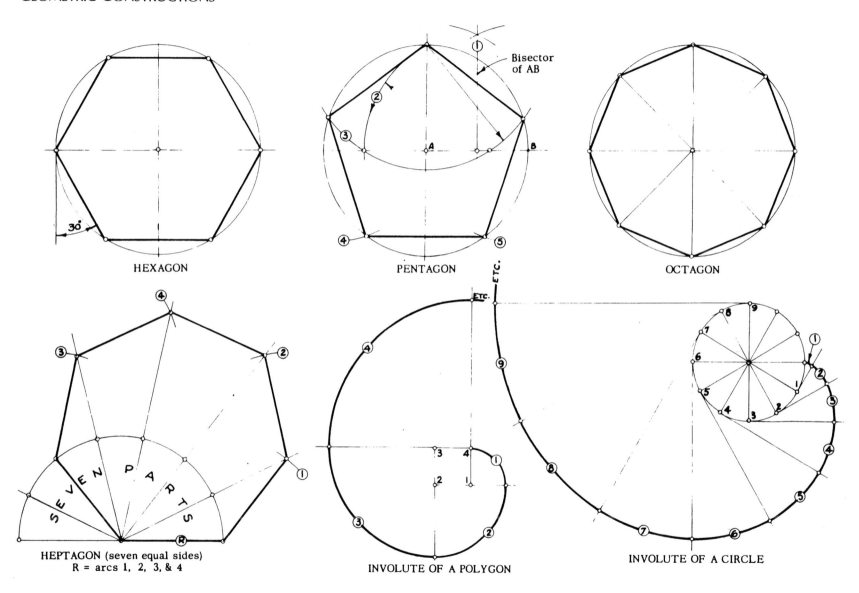

HEXAGON

PENTAGON

OCTAGON

HEPTAGON (seven equal sides)
R = arcs 1, 2, 3, & 4

INVOLUTE OF A POLYGON

INVOLUTE OF A CIRCLE

DIVIDING A LINE

Often it is desirable to divide a line into a number of equal parts. This is done by using the architects scale and triangles together to achieve the correct spacing.

 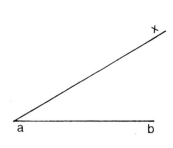 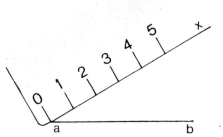 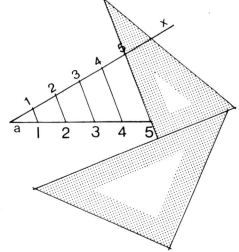

Given: Any line AB, divide into 5 equal parts.

Draw any line AX at any acute angle with AB.

Mark off five equal spaces, with any convenient scale, on line AX beginning at point A.

Draw a line from point 5 back to point B. Draw lines through the five points parallel to 5B. This divides AB into 5 equal spaces.

Types of Projection Drawing

Type		Classification	Projectors to Picture Plane	Projectors to Each Other	Relationship of Object to the Picture Plane
ORTHOGRAPHIC		MULTIVIEW	PERPENDICULAR	PARALLEL	FACES OF THE OBJECT ARE PARALLEL TO PICTURE PLANE
AXONOMETRIC		ISOMETRIC	PERPENDICULAR	PARALLEL	THE THREE AXES MAKE EQUAL ANGLES WITH PICTURE PLANE
		DIMETRIC	PERPENDICULAR	PARALLEL	THE TWO AXES MAKE EQUAL ANGLES WITH PICTURE PLANE
		TRIMETRIC	PERPENDICULAR	PARALLEL	ALL AXES MAKE DIFFERENT ANGLES WITH PICTURE PLANT
OBLIQUE		CAVALIER	OBLIQUE- ANY ANGLE	PARALLEL	ONE FACE PARALLEL TO THE PICTURE PLANE
		GENERAL	OBLIQUE- ANY ANGLE	PARALLEL	ONE FACE PARALLEL TO THE PICTURE PLANE
		CABINET	OBLIQUE- ANY ANGLE	PARALLEL	ONE FACE PARALLEL TO THE PICTURE PLANE
PERSPECTIVE		ONE-POINT	VARIOUS ANGLES	CONVERGE TO A POINT	ONE FACE PARALLEL TO THE PICTURE PLANE
		TWO-POINT	VARIOUS ANGLES	CONVERGE TO A POINT	VERTICAL FACES AT ANGLE WITH PICTURE PLANE

CHAPTER 3

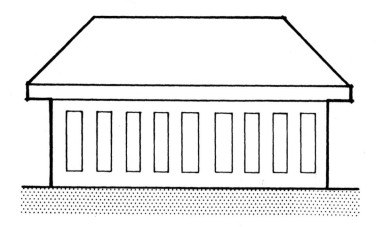

ORTHOGRAPHIC PROJECTION

Orthographic Projection

Illustrated below in pictorial form is the system of ORTHOGRAPHIC PROJECTION showing the relationships of picture planes and the object plus the various resultant images of each projection. The theory of this system will be explained in further detail in this chapter.

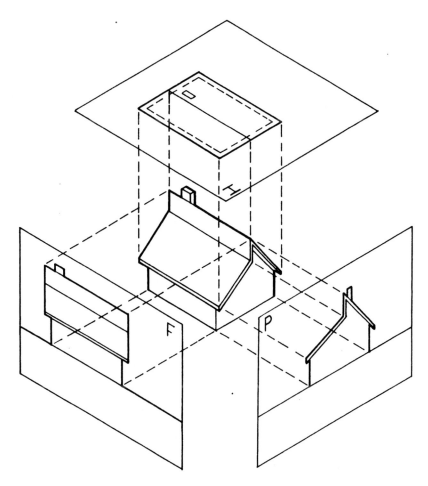

ORTHOGRAPHIC PROJECTION

In order for a building to become a reality, it is first necessary to communicate architectural and technical data about the building in a logical manner. This requires a method or system of communication which is easy to use and understand. Such a system is the practice of making drawings on imaginary picture planes which illustrate various parts of the intended building. These planes are considered transparent and are placed between the observer and the object. In order for the system to work, all lines of sight from the observer to the object are perpendicular to these planes. This method of drawing is called **Orthographic Projection** and can be defined as a system of drawing where the image of an object is projected on a series of picture planes by parallel projectors from the object perpendicular to the picture plane. The system of orthographic projection is illustrated below in pictorial form.

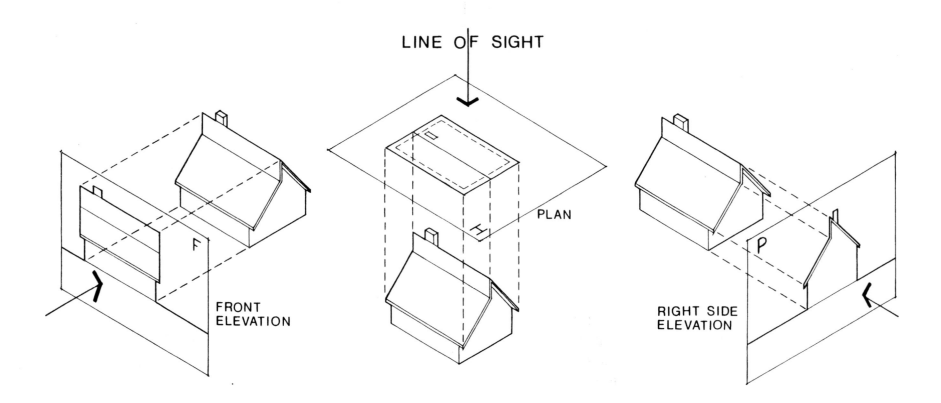

LINE OF SIGHT

PLAN

F

FRONT
ELEVATION

RIGHT SIDE
ELEVATION

P

Three principal planes of projection are used in orthographic projection. They are: Horizontal, Frontal, Profile or Side, and all are placed perpendicular to each other to form a 90° system. The example on the left shows the imaginary principal planes folded together in pictorial. This pictorial illustrates the position of the principal planes to each other and the object being communicated. The drawing on the right illustrates how the planes are unfolded to lie in one flat plane. The common lines between the planes which are used to unfold the system are called "hinge lines" and separate the principal views from each other.

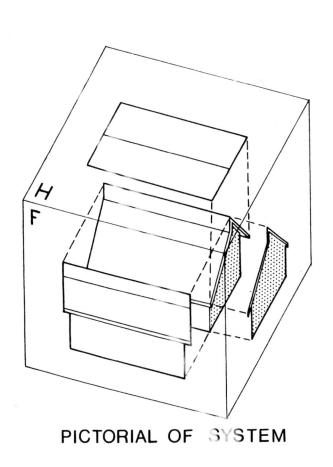

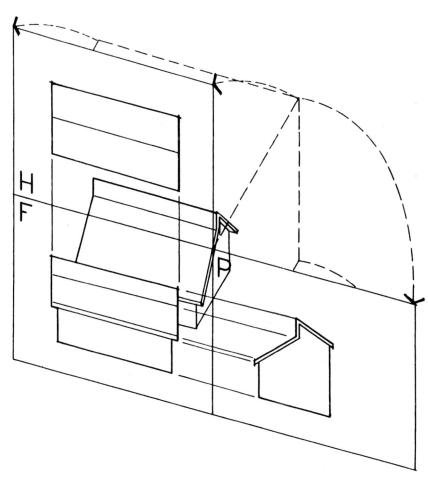

PICTORIAL OF SYSTEM

UNFOLDING THE PLANES OF PROJECTION

PRINCIPLE VIEWS

The example on the left illustrates the principal planes of projection (H, F, P) unfolded to form a multiview drawing in orthographic. Note the common lines between the planes are called "hinge lines" and separate the views from each other. The illustration on the right removes the boundaries of the principal planes leaving only the "hinge lines" for reference. This is the usual standard for most orthographic drawings and is especially true when working problems in descriptive geometry.

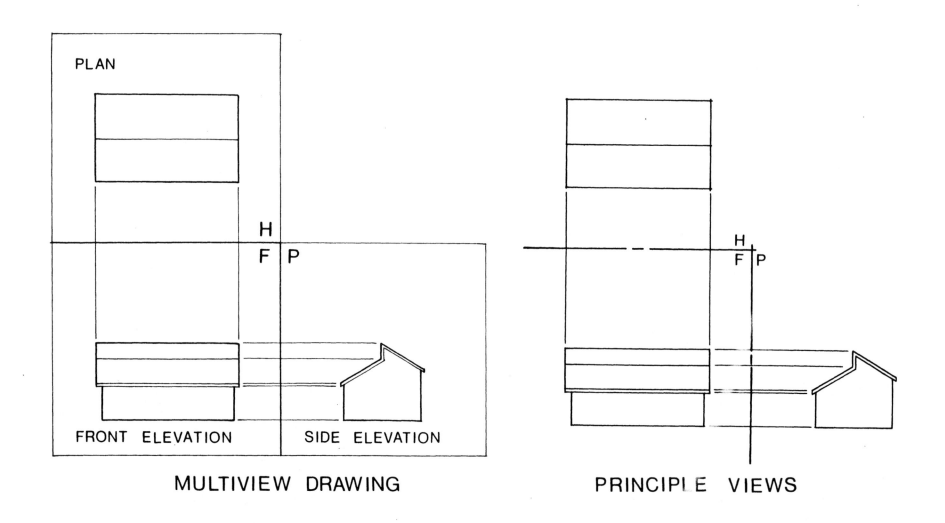

MULTIVIEW DRAWING   PRINCIPLE VIEWS

In architecture, it is a standard practice to isolate the individual views and draw them out of projection with each other. This is done because the size of the drawing doesn't permit keeping them in strict orthographic alignment since they would not fit on a standard size sheet of paper. Also note that in some cases the elevation views are labeled by a compass direction which is determined by the placement of the building from North and the direction each facade faces. Thus a view labeled North Elevation means that the portion illustrated faces North. Likewise the East Elevation faces East, the South Elevation faces South, and the West Elevation faces West. Other terms often used are: front, rear, back, and side which help to distinguish each elevation and also places them in context with the plan.

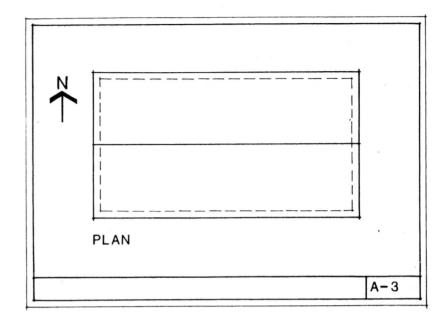

PLAN

A-3

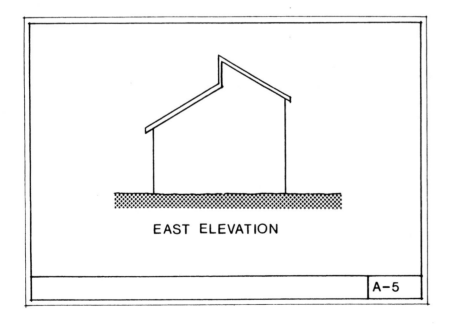

EAST ELEVATION

A-5

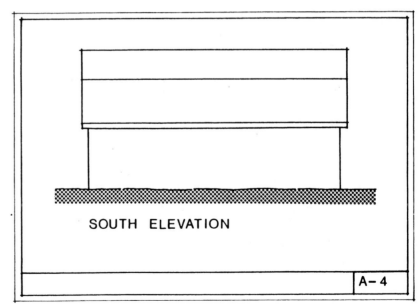

SOUTH ELEVATION

A-4

The system of orthographic projection which is used to convey information about an object, is best understood when the object is described in terms of points, lines, and planes. An analysis of this type will allow for a simple method of communication, and is easier to visualize when performing certain basic projections. In order to become acquainted with the system of orthographic projection, the theory of projecting points is illustrated.

Where the imaginary planes of projection intersect they form a line called a "hinge line." This reference line allows for the proper alignment and correct relationship of principal views. In the projection of points, it is important to note the following with respect to the "hinge line."

1. All views are in proper alignment, with the plan and front views aligned vertically, and the front and side views aligned horizontally. When aligned in this manner, the views are called "in projection."

2. The plan view is labeled "H," the front view is labeled "F," and the profile view is labeled "P." All points projected on any of these reference planes are labeled with the same letter notation.

3. Each "hinge line" represents the intersection of two adjacent planes of projection which are seen as edges in one of the given views. For example, when looking at the front view, the H/F hinge line represents the horizontal plane seen as an edge. When looking at the plan view, this same H/F hinge line represents the frontal plane as an edge. The same convention is consistent for the F/P hinge line. Thus one is able to coordinate dimensions from the principal planes of projection, and this will allow for the use of auxiliary views.

The chart on the next page illustrates the relationship that exists between choice of view and the corresponding reference plane as seen as an edge. When the reference plane is seen as an edge, appropriate distances can be measured in relationship to it. For example, using the chart as a guide, when looking down from the top into the horizontal view allows one to see the Frontal Reference plane as an edge which means distances can be measured behind the Frontal Plane because in the top view it appears as an edge. Thus a study of each view will show a corresponding reference plane appearing as an edge which allows for direct measuring. It is important to note that each view selected provides a unique view (plan, elevation) as well as possible edge views for measuring.

PICTORIAL VS ORTHOGRAPHIC

Selected View "V"	Reference Plane Seen as Edge	Allows Measuring	Pictorial vs Orthographic	
FRONT	HORIZONTAL	BELOW "H"		MEASURE BELOW "H"
FRONT	PROFILE	LEFT OF "P"		MEASURE LEFT OF "P"
HORIZONTAL OR TOP	FRONTAL	BEHIND "F"		MEASURE BEHIND "F"
PROFILE OR SIDE	FRONTAL	BEHIND "F"		MEASURE BEHIND "F"
PROFILE OR SIDE	HORIZONTAL	BELOW "H"		MEASURE BELOW "H"

PROJECTION OF POINTS

The projection of points is a necessary prerequisite for the understanding of orthographic projection. The following four illustrations on this page and the next show the sequential steps in plotting point "A" which lies: 1 unit below H

½ unit left of P

¾ unit behind F

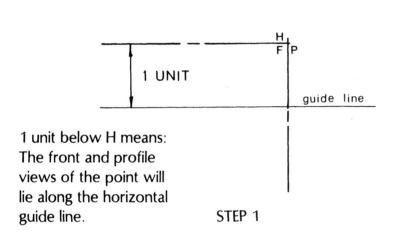

1 unit below H means:
The front and profile views of the point will lie along the horizontal guide line.

STEP 1

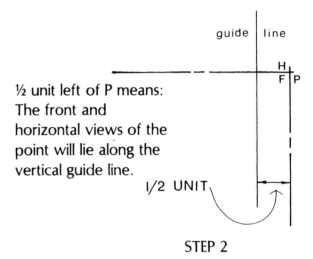

½ unit left of P means:
The front and horizontal views of the point will lie along the vertical guide line.

STEP 2

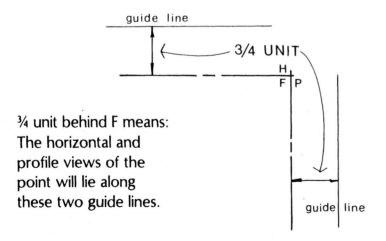

¾ unit behind F means:
The horizontal and profile views of the point will lie along these two guide lines.

STEP 3

Combining all three views produces a multiview drawing of point "A" which illustrates its relative position with respect to the three principal planes of projection (H, F, P).
Note use of subscripts for proper labeling and helpful identificaiton.

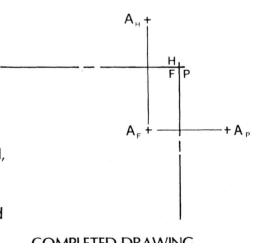

COMPLETED DRAWING
LOCATING POINT "A"

PROJECTION OF POINTS

The two examples on this page illustrate the correct method of locating a point in orthographic projection given specific coordinate dimensions.

Point "B" has the following coordinate dimensions: 1 unit behind F
2 units below H
3 units left of P

Point "C" has the following coordinate dimensions: 1 unit behind F
2 units left of P
On H

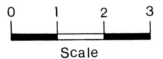

Scale

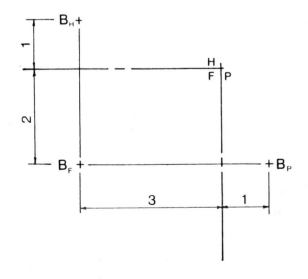

POINT "B"

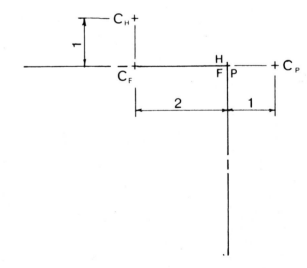

POINT "C"

AUXILIARY VIEWS

In a set of architectural drawings, it is important to provide complete information regarding the building and its construction. This usually requires drawing many views of the building such as plans, elevations, and sections. Thus the three principal orthographic views of plan, front and side elevations may not be enough to completely describe the building in adequate detail. In this case, auxiliary views are often required to supplement existing data. Such views can be classified as Auxiliary Elevation, Inclined, or Oblique. The examples given below illustrate the various types of auxiliary views.

An auxiliary Elevation View is any auxiliary view which shows the horizontal plane as an edge.

An auxiliary Inclined View is any auxiliary view showing either the frontal or profile planes as edges.

An Oblique View is any auxiliary view which is skew to the principal planes. It is often adjacent to an auxiliary plane or another oblique plane.

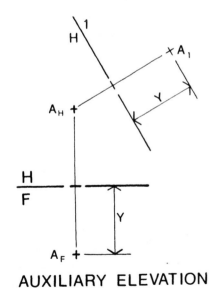

AUXILIARY ELEVATION

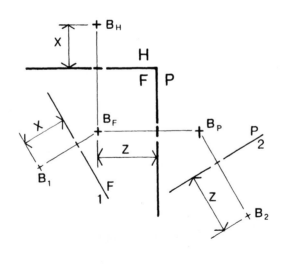

AUXILIARY INCLINED

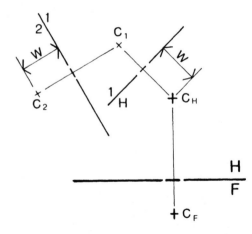

AUXILIARY OBLIQUE

An illustration of Auxiliary
Elevation, Auxiliary Inclined and Principal
Views.

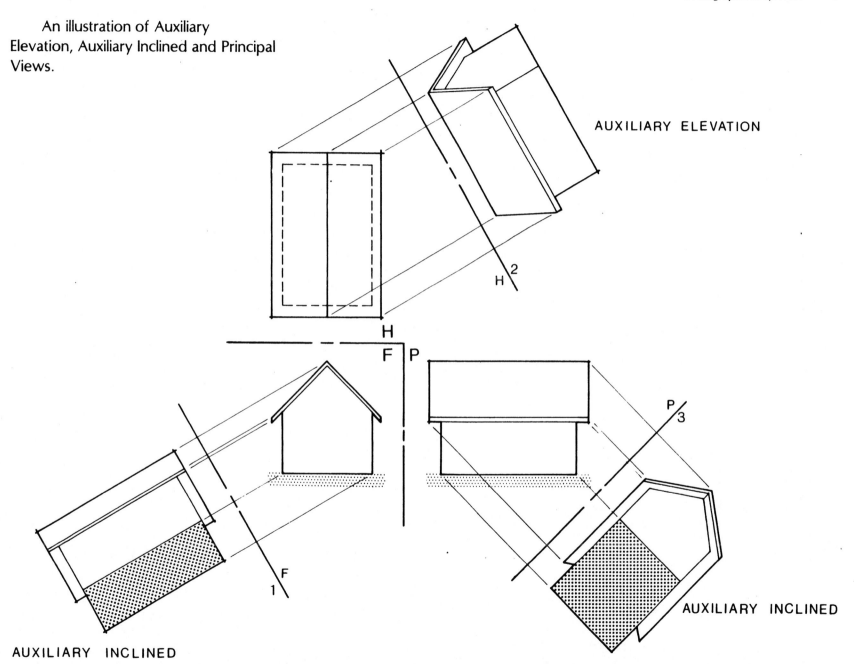

AUXILIARY ELEVATION

AUXILIARY INCLINED

AUXILIARY INCLINED

The easiest method for learning the theory of orthographic projection is to project a point form view to view, especially auxiliary views. When considering this method, remember that each view is of the same point and that the observer has changed positions in order to look at the point from a different angle. The choice and position of auxiliary views will be determined later when projecting lines and planes. When constructing each new view, attention should be paid to projection alignment with respect to reference planes and that appropriate distances are used for measurements.

The illustrations below show the step by step layout of a point through a series of auxiliary views.

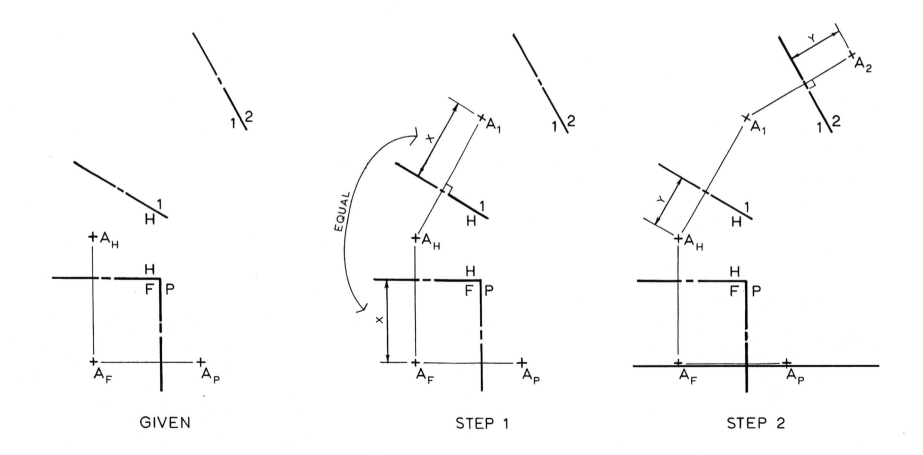

GIVEN   STEP 1   STEP 2

CLASSIFICATION OF LINES

In the orthographic projection of lines, several basic projections are important to understand in order to use the system to its potential. Such projections are: Classification, True Length, Inclination, Point View, and Bearing. With respect to the first, lines can be classified as follows:

A Horizontal line is one that is parallel to the horizontal reference plane.

Frontal line is one that is parallel to the frontal reference plane.

Profile line is one that is parallel to the profile reference plane.

Oblique line is one that is oblique to all three principal reference planes.

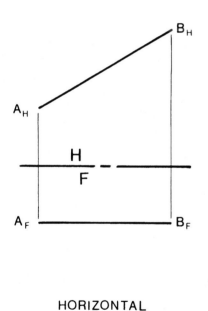

HORIZONTAL

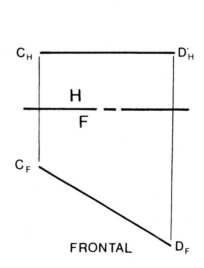

FRONTAL

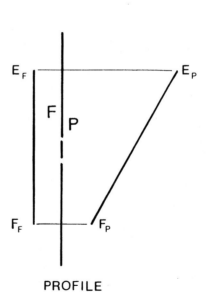

PROFILE

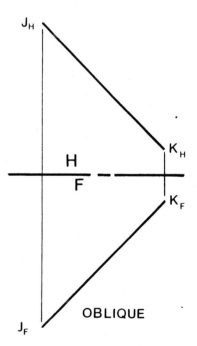

OBLIQUE

CLASSIFICATION OF LINES

Additional classification of lines that meet "special" cases or combination of classifications are as follows:

A Vertical line is both parallel to the frontal and profile reference planes. It also appears as a point in the plan view.

A Horizontal/Frontal line appears parallel to both reference planes. Thus it contains a combination of two terms.

The Horizontal/Profile line appears as a point view in the front view. Don't confuse it with the vertical line.

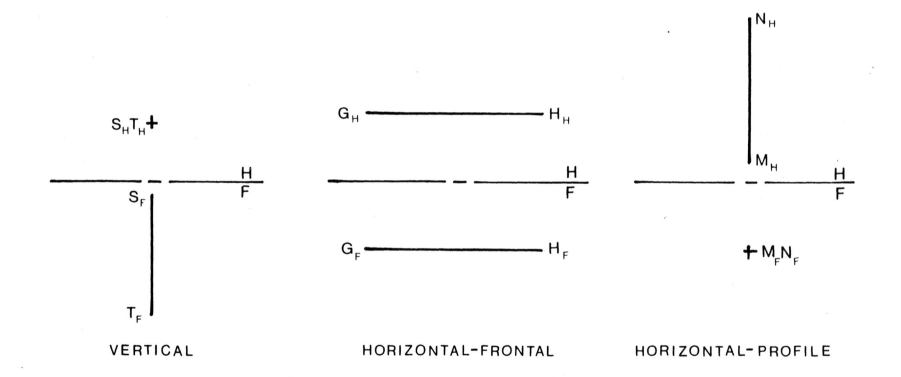

VERTICAL   HORIZONTAL-FRONTAL   HORIZONTAL-PROFILE

BEARING OF A LINE

The bearing of a line is measured in the plan view of the line and is its deviation from north to south measured in degrees. The angle of bearing will always be an acute angle and always measured in the plan view. Whenever possible, the direction of north is placed toward the top of the page. Lines which are positioned north/south or east/west are called Due North or Due south and Due East or Due West.

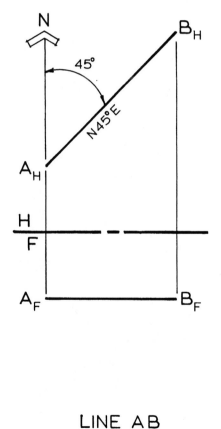

LINE AB

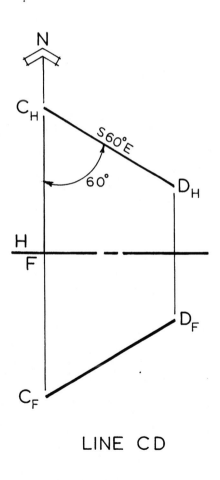

LINE CD

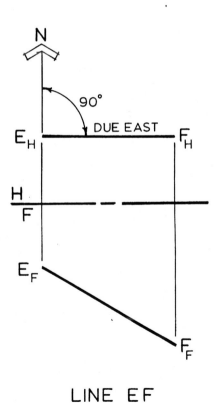

LINE EF

TRUE LENGTH

The true length of a line will appear on a plane of projection that is parallel to the line. This may be seen in a principal view if the line has the correct position, or in an auxiliary view if the line is classified as oblique. In the illustrations below, the lines are true length in the plan view, front view and right profile view. It is important to note the orientation and alignment of each line and the parallel relationship that exists between true length projection and adjacent views.

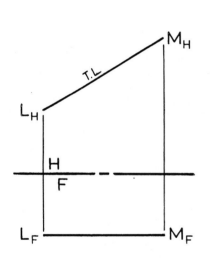 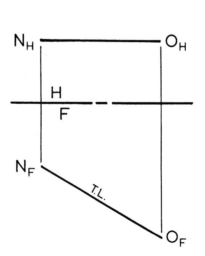 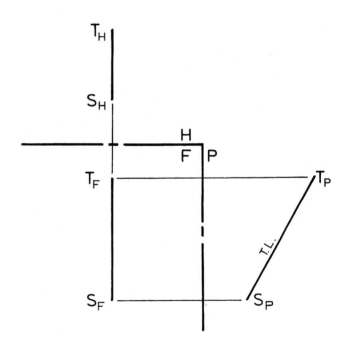

TRUE LENGTH IN AUXILIARY VIEWS

Often it is necessary to obtain the true length of a line. Sometimes the line will appear true length in the given orthographic views. When this takes place, it is only necessary to identify and measure the line segment. The true length of a line will appear on a plane of projection that is parallel to the line. For example, a horizontal line will appear true length in the plan view because the horizontal reference plane is parallel to the line in the front view. In the examples below, each line appears parallel to a particular reference plane and in turn is true length in an adjacent related view.

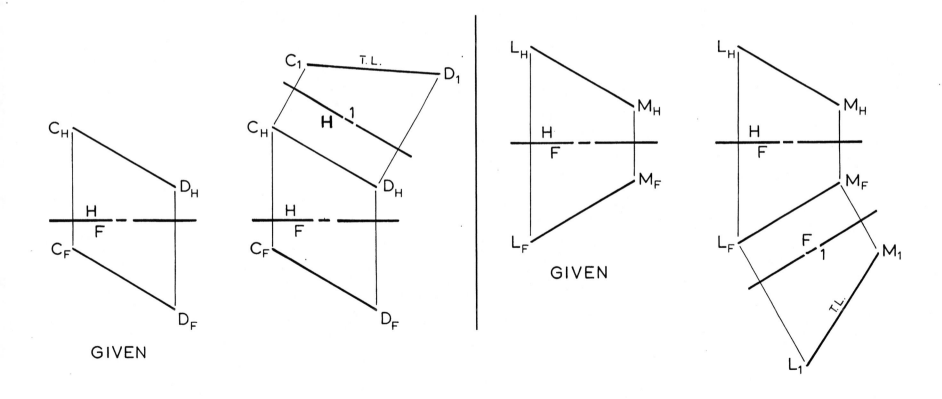

GIVEN

GIVEN

INCLINATION OF LINES

The inclination of a line is its deviation from horizontal and is expressed in a variety of ways depending upon use. In order to see the exact angle of inclination, the line must be seen in a true length elevation view. Thus it may be possible to measure inclination in the principal front and profile views or may require an auxiliary elevation view in the case of an oblique line.

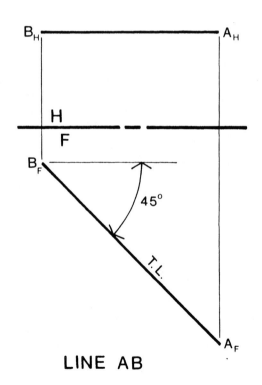

LINE AB

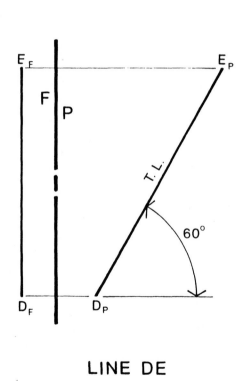

LINE DE

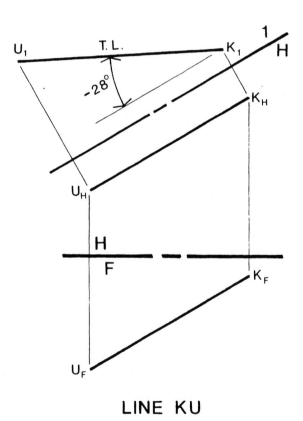

LINE KU

INCLINATION OF LINES

The problem illustrated below shows how to determine the Bearing, Inclination, and True Length of a line that is classified as oblique. In solving the problem, an auxillary elevation view is required in order to accurately measure the slope angle of the line as it appears in true length.

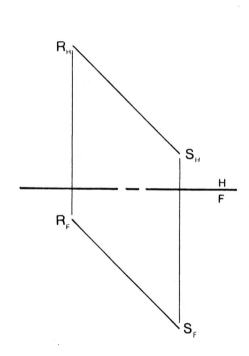

GIVEN PROBLEM

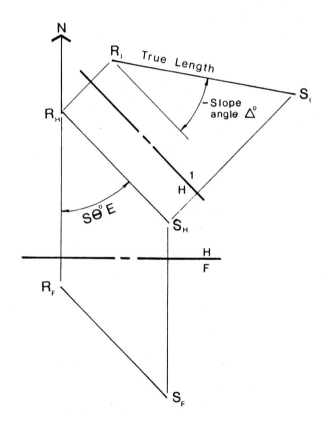

SOLUTION:
Bearing $= S\theta° E$
Slope Angle $= -\Delta°$
True Length $=$ In Auxillary View

LINE DATA

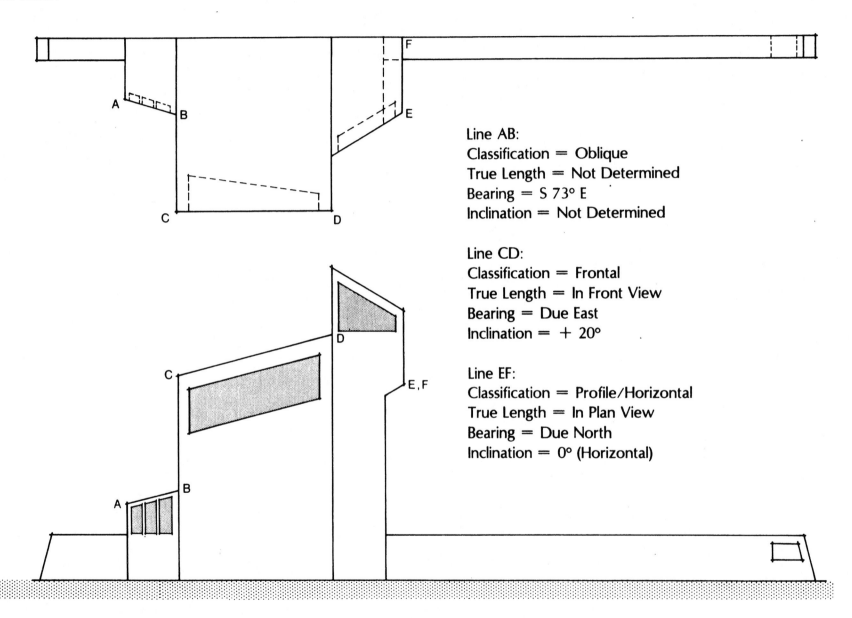

Line AB:
Classification = Oblique
True Length = Not Determined
Bearing = S 73° E
Inclination = Not Determined

Line CD:
Classification = Frontal
True Length = In Front View
Bearing = Due East
Inclination = + 20°

Line EF:
Classification = Profile/Horizontal
True Length = In Plan View
Bearing = Due North
Inclination = 0° (Horizontal)

Inclination

   The inclination of lines and planes is measured in a elevation view showing the line in true length or the plane as **an edge.** Although the different expressions of inclination have particular applications, they are often interchanged.

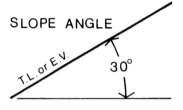

SLOPE ANGLE

T.L. or E.V.

30°

Definition: The Vertical Angle. Dihedral Angle for Planes.
Expression: Degrees (Angle with the Horizontal Plane)
Application: General Usage
Example: 30°

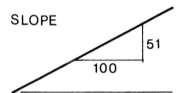

SLOPE

51

100

Definition: Rise/Run or Tangent of Slope Angle
Expression: Decimal
Application: Drainage and Slope of Ground in Contours
Example: Rise/Run = 51/100 = 0.51

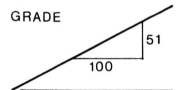

GRADE

51

100

Definition: Rise/Run
Expression: Percent
Application: Plot Grading and Roadways
Example: Rise/Run = 51/100 = 51%

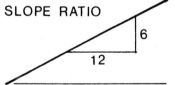

SLOPE RATIO

6

12

Definition: Rise/Run
Expression: Ratio with 12 for the Longer, Rise or Run
Application: Structural Members, Roof, and Stairways
Example: 6/12

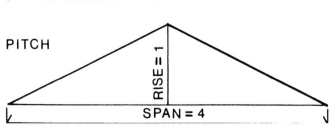

PITCH

RISE = 1

SPAN = 4

Definition: Rise/Span (Rise Will Always Be 1)
Expression: Ratio of 1/Span
Application: Roofs and Trusses
Example: Rise/Span = 1/4

POINT VIEW OF A LINE

Obtaining a view showing a line as a point is a necessary maneuver useful when obtaining information about planes. Before the orthographic projection of a line as a point can be found, it is first necessary to find the true length view. After this is determined, a plane is then positioned perpendicular to the true length view such that the resultant projection gives a point of view of the line. The key to understanding the system of orthographic projection using auxiliary views is to remember that each successive auxiliary plane is perpendicular to the preceding plane. One should also be able to visualize where to take appropriate measurements for the distances needed to draw the auxiliary views.

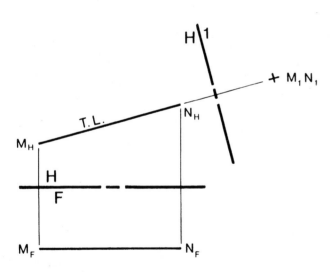 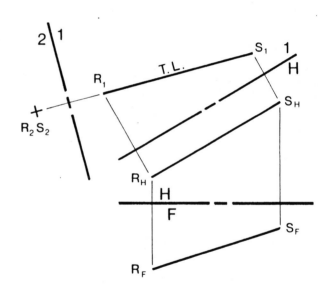

POINT VIEW OF A LINE

Drawing a Line from Specifications

It is often necessary to construct a line which has certain specifications such as the bearing, true length, and inclination. This usually requires a three step procedure which is: (1) Draw the correct bearing of the line. (2) Using an auxiliary elevation view, draw in the proper inclination. (3) In the auxiliary view measure the true length of the line and project back to all views. The example shown has the following specifications: Bearing = N 30° W, Inclination = −25°, True Length = 1 1/2".

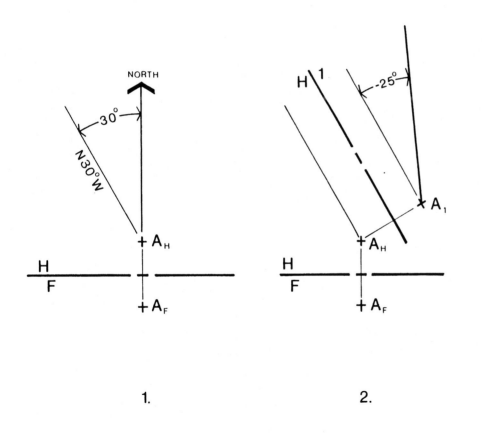

1.

2.

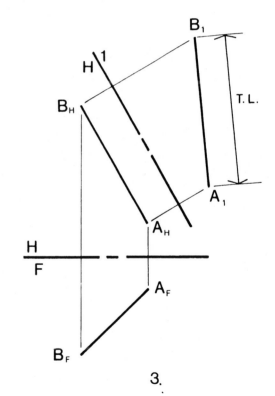

3.

PROJECTION OF PLANES

In the orthographic projection of planes, one begins to see the true value of having a system of projection. Architecturally, planes provide the architect with a method of expressing a product and thus it is of utmost importance that they are understood. Specifically, a minimum of three points not in a straight line determine a plane. Other ways to represent a plane are: parallel lines, a line and a point not on the line, and intersecting lines. For reasons of simplicity and expediency, a plane represented by three points connected to form a triangle will be used to illustrate the basic projections.

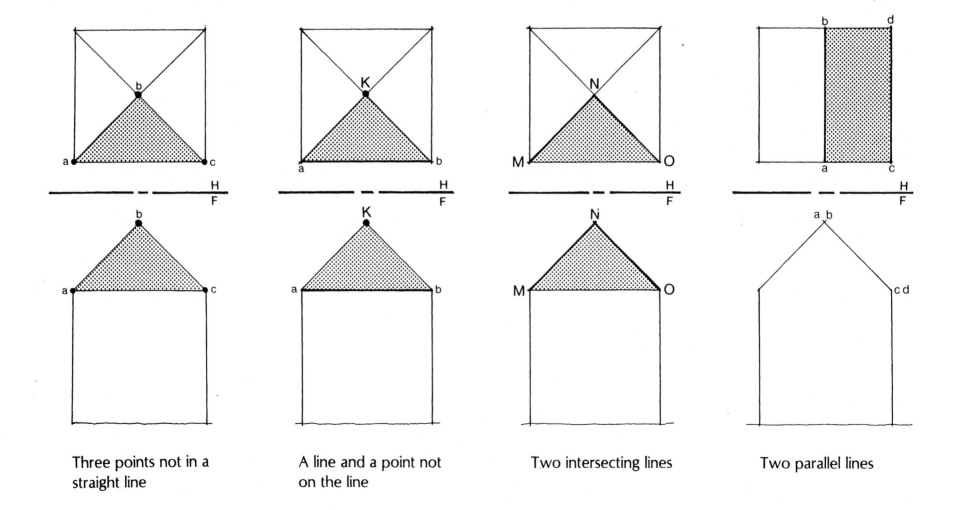

Three points not in a straight line

A line and a point not on the line

Two intersecting lines

Two parallel lines

POINTS AND LINES ON PLANES

Two basic projections involving planes are: placing a point on any plane in space, and placing a line on any plane. These fundamental projections are presented at this time in order to graphically maneuver planes when auxiliary views are required.

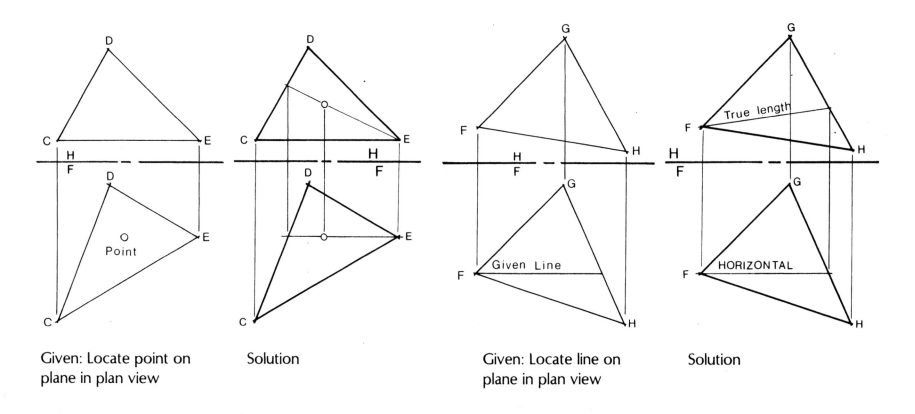

Given: Locate point on   Solution   Given: Locate line on   Solution
plane in plan view   plane in plan view

LINES AND PLANES

Two additional basic projections with respect to planes are: drawing a line perpendicular to any plane, and passing a cutting-plane through a given plane and locating its line of intersection. Both of these concepts require special consideration because they are fundamental projections which are often employed in the study of architecture.

Drawing a line perpendicular to any plane. If a line is perpendicular to a plane, it will appear at right angles to any line on the plane that shows in true length.

Passing a cutting-plane through a given plane. The cutting-plane is positioned and will appear as an edge so that it will project a resultant line of intersection in the adjacent view.

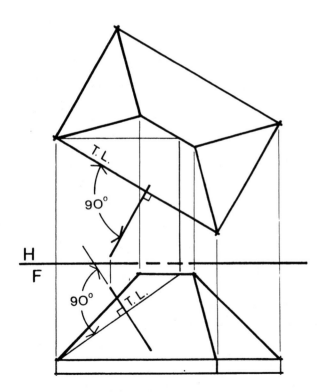

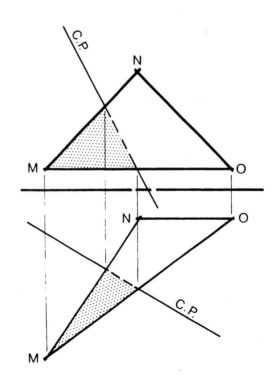

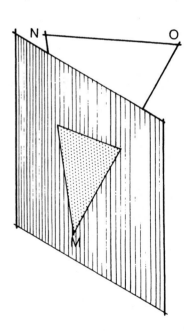

INCLINATION OF PLANES

Measuring the inclination of a roof is an essential and standard procedure in architecture. It is generally done in a elevation view because here the roof plane will often appear as an edge. In some cases, the plane in question will not be seen as an edge in any of the elevation views, and it is then necessary to auxiliary projection to obtain the required information. To become proficient in projecting planes that are not conveniently situated, that is, have and edge view in one of the elevation views, it is necessary to project the plane into such a position that its inclination can be seen and measured. As a rule, the inclination of a plane can only be measured where the plane appears as an edge in a elevation view.

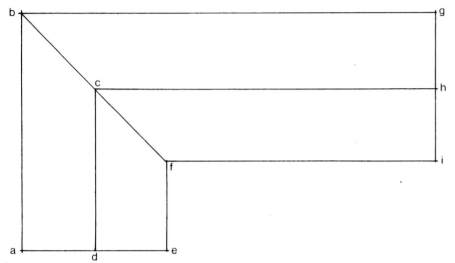

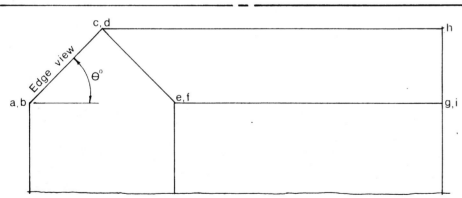

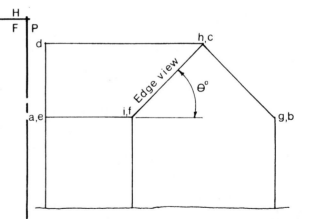

In the front view planes abcd and cdef appear as edges thus the inclination of the planes can be measured.

In the profile view planes chfi and cbgh appear as edges thus their inclination can be measured in this view.

INCLINATION OF PLANES

Plane STU is in such a position that it does not appear as an edge in either the front or profile views. Thus in order to determine the inclination of the plane it is necessary to view the plane as an edge in an auxiliary elevation view. The procedure for doing this is illustrated below.

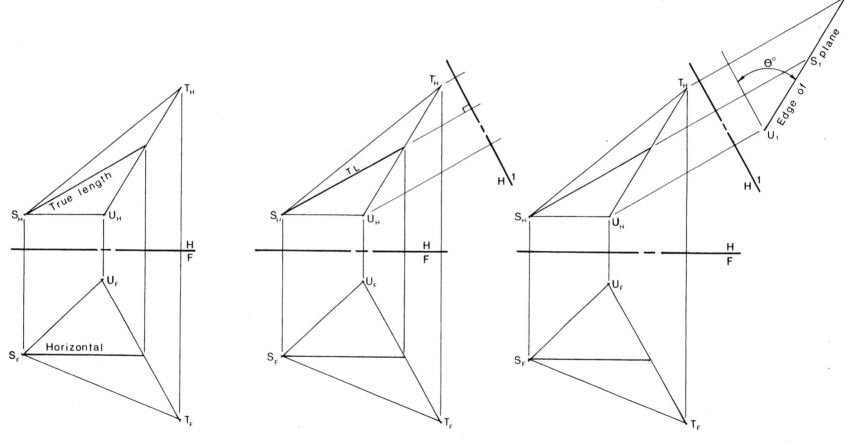

Step 1: Locate any horizontal line on the plane in the front view and find the corresponding horizontal projection of the line which will be in true length.

Step 2: Construct an auxiliary elevation view perpendicular to the true length line in plan.

Step 3: Project the edge view of the plane in the auxiliary view and measure the inclination from horizontal.

TRUE SIZE OF A PLANE

In order to detail a building, it is essential to know the true size and shape of many different parts of the proposed structure. It would be difficult to estimate the cost of the building or detail its construction, if one did not know how to determine the true shape of certain areas. The graphic procedure for finding the true size of a plane is to first locate an edge view either in a principal view or by means of auxiliary views, and then project a view normal to the edge view.

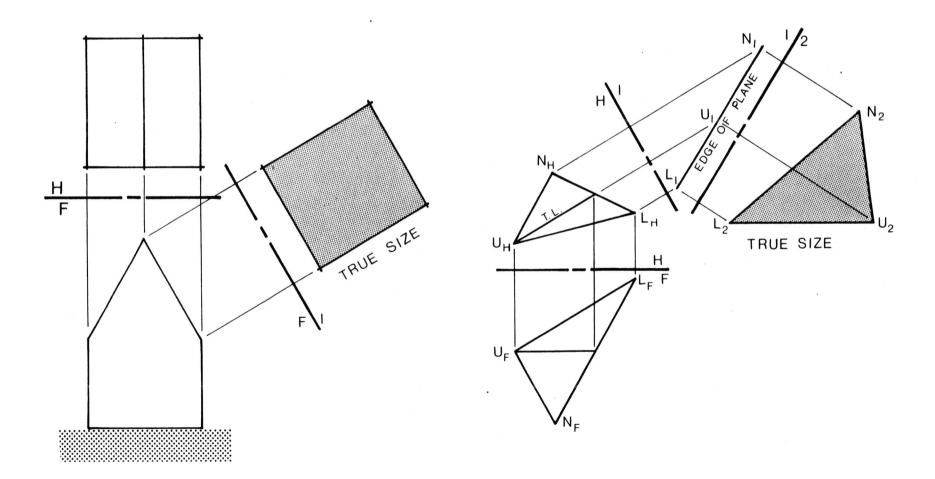

An example of finding the true shape of a plane using auxiliary projection.

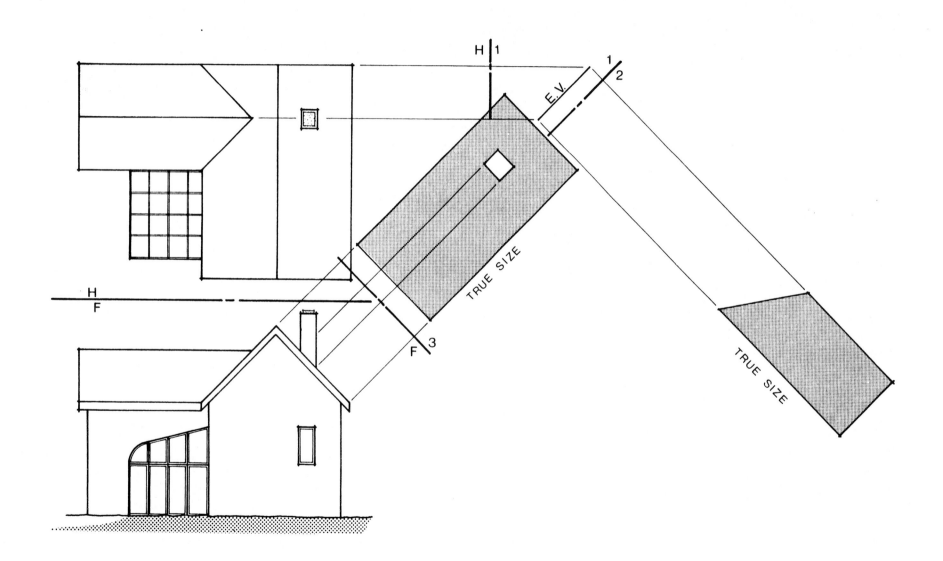

Dihedral Angle

In architecture, it is important to know how to find the true shape and size of various planes, but perhaps even more important, is determining the dihedral angle between two planes. This becomes obvious when one considers the number of possibilities for joining different roof systems together. Thus the dihedral angle is a important application in architectural detailing. The angle can be measured in a view that shows both planes as edges. This is possible by finding the line of intersection of the planes as a point.

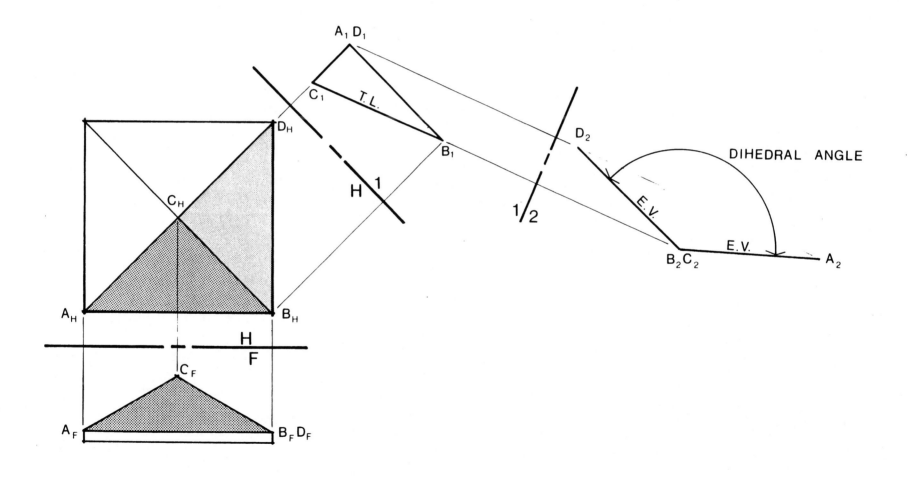

ANGLE BETWEEN A LINE AND PLANE

Often an architect will be required to determine the angle between a line and a plane. This problem may at first hand sound rather easy to accomplish but becomes complex when it becomes apparent that the angle can only be measured where the line shows in true length and the plane as an edge. In the case of an oblique line and plane, the procedure is to remember that any view projected from a true shape view of a plane will again show an edge view, thus the last auxiliary view must be chosen so that the line shows in true length. Note, in the final step the 2/3 hinge line is placed parallel to the line QU so that the line will be in true length in the final view.

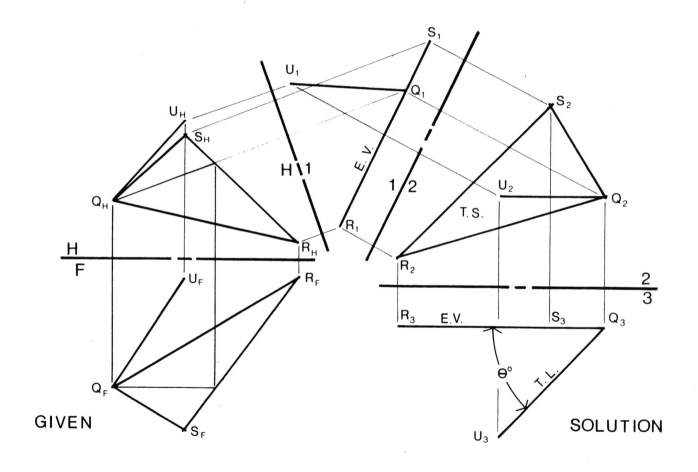

PIERCING POINT OF A LINE AND PLANE

When designing a building, the architect is often confronted with the problem of determining the piercing point of a line and plane. Several methods are available for solving the problem. They are as follows:

1. A view of the line and the plane, where the plane is shown as an edge.

2. A view of the line and the plane, where the line is shown as a point.

3. Passing a cutting-plane through the given line and locating intersecting lines.

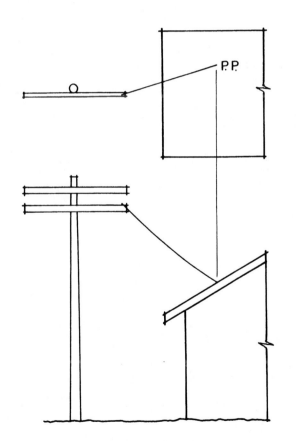

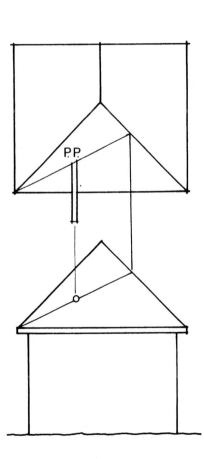

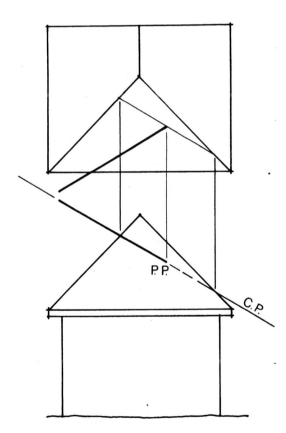

The following problem illustrates the solution for finding the piercing point between a line and a plane.

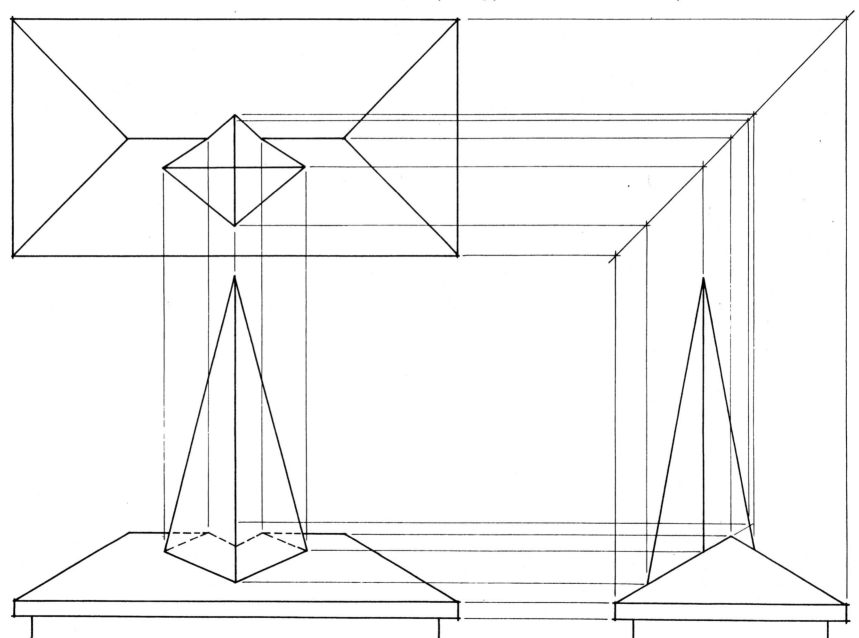

LINE OF INTERSECTION

Finding the line of intersection between two planes is an important concept in architecture. If one is limited by his ability to design only those structures in which the obvious line of intersection can be found, then he is limiting his design potential considerably. When the line of intersection between two planes is not shown, it can be determined by several methods.

Plane as an edge method. A view of both planes showing one plane as an edge will show the line of intersection between the two planes.

Cutting-plane method. By passing a cutting-plane through both of the given planes, the two lines of intersection will intersect to locate one point on the new line of intersection between the two planes. This method is repeated again until two points are found on the common line of intersection.

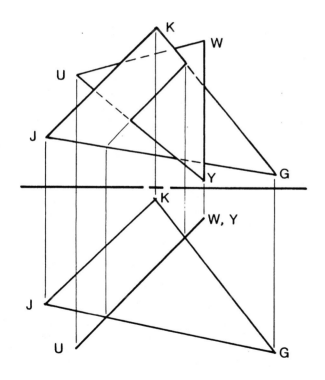

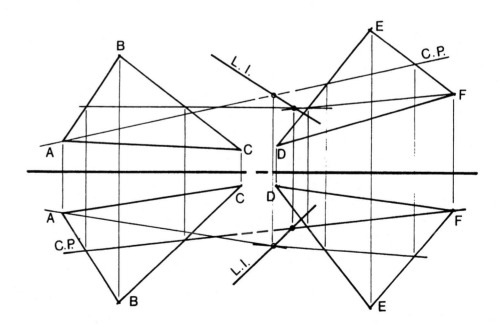

CHAPTER 4

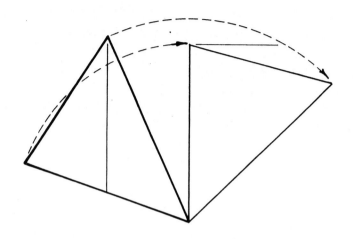

PROBLEM SOLUTIONS
BY ROTATION

ROTATION OF LINES

Often it will be advantageous to solve problems using another method of orthographic projection which is more convenient than the standard method of auxiliary views which requires the observer to move his line of sight for each view desired. Many different views can also be obtained by rotating the object. Thus the observer remains fixed, while the object is rotated about an axis until the desired information is found. When using this method, several fundamental principles must be observed:

1. An axis of rotation must be identified and located before the object is rotated.
2. Where the axis shows as a point view the object will change position during rotation but will not change size or shape. Likewise, those dimensions which are in the true length projection of the axis will remain constant.

These principles are illustrated below finding the true length and point view of lines.

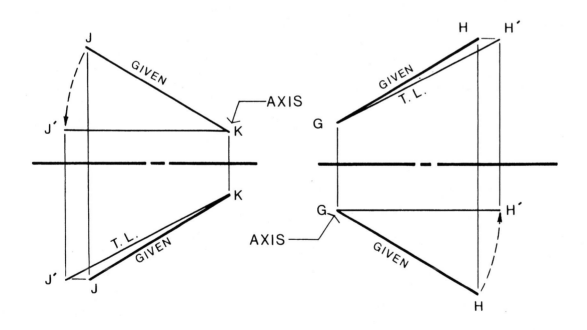

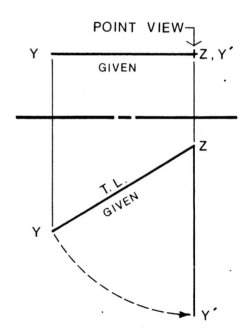

ROTATION OF A PLANE

The illustration below shows how to use double rotation to find the edge view and true shape of a plane. Although the method of rotation eliminates some of the auxiliary views associated with standard projection, its use in solving complicated problems is limited because of the tendency to overlap during rotation.

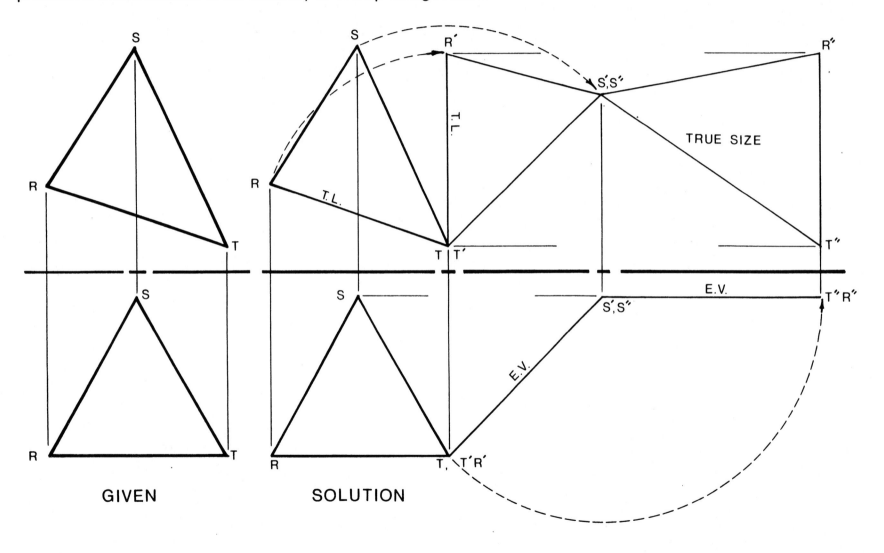

GIVEN   SOLUTION

ROTATION OF LINES AND PLANES

Using rotation to find: (1) the shortest distance between two lines and, (2) the inclination of a plane.

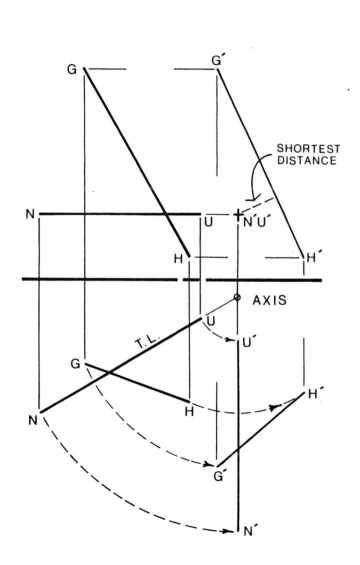

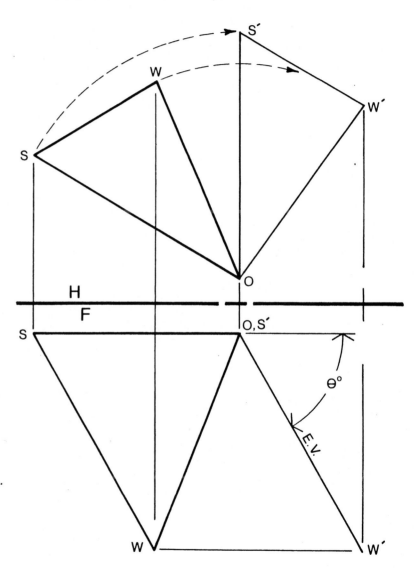

CHAPTER 5

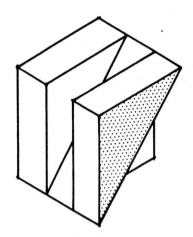

PROJECTION OF SOLIDS

PROJECTION OF SOLIDS

Up to this point, the discussion of orthographic projection has concentrated on points, lines, and planes. The projection of solid architectural objects is also treated similarly to that of points, lines, or planes, since any object can be reduced to these basic elements. As determined previously, the conventional position and alignment of the principal views are such that the side elevations are adjacent to the front elevation which in turn is hinged to the plan. These standard views are so arranged to provide complete shape description and the purpose of any orthographic drawing is to completely describe the object in a minimum number of views. Thus, the number of views is a function of the complexity of the object and may vary from one view for a simple design while more intricate problems might require more than the normal principal views.

In order to fully illustrate a design in orthographic, hidden lines are used to indicate those details which are invisible. Such details are represented on the drawing with dashed lines. Centerlines are also used to indicate the axes of symmetry and aid in the location of center points of circles. Because of the various types of lines employed in orthographic drawing, the following rule is used as a method for determining the proper hierarchy when lines are superimposed. Outlines take precedence over centerlines and hidden lines, and hidden lines take precedence over centerlines.

One should be reminded that in order to have a drawing which conveys an architectural character, proper line quality and delineation must be employed. Object lines are bold, centerlines are light and delicate, and hidden lines are usually lighter than object lines with the dashes uniform in length and spacing.

VISUALIZATION

The following problems illustrate the importance of using a third view to describe an object. Also, line precedence is employed as a method for solving the problems and making them possible.

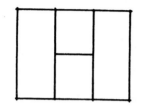

Five possible right profile views that are correct for the given plan and front view.

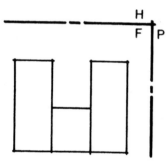
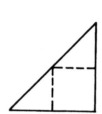
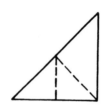
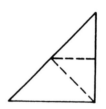
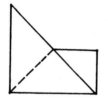

Two possible right profile views that are correct for the given plan and front view.

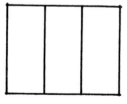
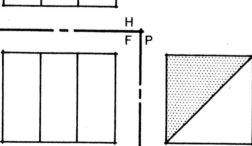
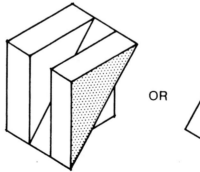

OR

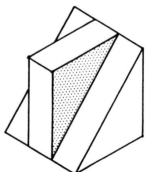

PROJECTION OF SOLIDS

Illustrated below is an example of projecting a object into trimetric projection. Other types of axonometric projections are discussed in Chapter 8 on Pictorial Drawings.

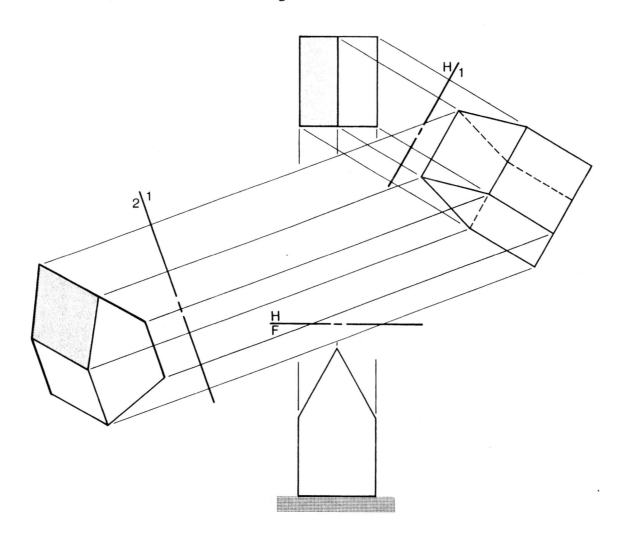

CHAPTER **6**

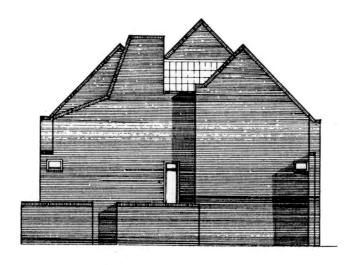

DRAWING CONVENTIONS

DRAWING CONVENTIONS

With respect to orthographic projection, the architect is concerned with a variety of methods of architectural presentation based upon the use and intent of the drawings. For example, are the drawings intended for explaining architectural concepts to another architect or client, or are the drawings to be used as construction documents to aid those who will build the design? Each situation suggests a style of drawing activity which will dictate an appropriate method of communication. The following two types of drawing conventions are most often used in architectural practice.

1. Presentation Drawings. These drawings suggest the character and spatial qualities of the intended design and usually consist of the following drawings: plans, elevations, sections, and pictorials. They are useful in conveying to the client information about the circulation, spatial qualities, structure, form, color, and texture of the building. Specific details of construction are generally not illustrated in these drawings as the intent is to communicate a concept. See Chapter 13 for methods of constructing these types of drawings.

2. Production Drawings or Working Drawings. These drawings are for illustrating how the building is constructed and are intended for use by those in the construction industry. The drawings should be detailed enough so that information required by the contractor is sufficient enough to complete the building exactly as specified by the architect. A typical set of production drawings would include the following:

1. Site Plan with Sheet Schedule
2. Foundation Plan and Details
3. Floor Plans and Schedules
4. Elevations
5. Sections and Details
6. Miscellaneous Details

Presentation Drawings are often done on illustration boards where a method of color can be applied. They usually have the title of the design along with simple notes so that the client can visualize the concepts of the scheme. Often they will be used as a method to generate discussion, so that the total design project can be understood and communicated.

Production Drawings are first done on tracing paper or special paper and then "prints" are duplicated for distribution to the various building interests. Several photochemical printing methods are available such as blueprints, diazo, and Van Dyke. All of these methods duplicate the original drawing for easy distribution and handling.

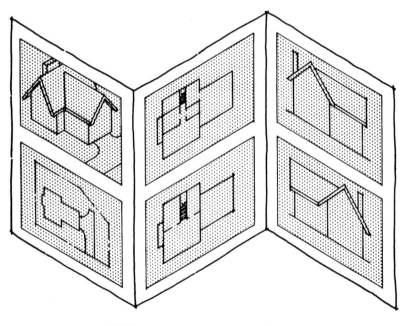

PRESENTATION DRAWINGS

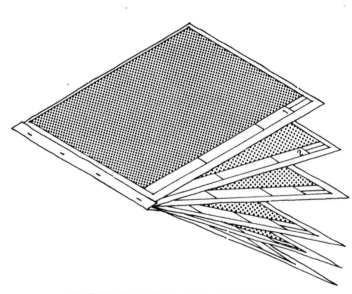

PRODUCTION DRAWINGS

SITE PLANS

As suggested earlier, two types of drawing conventions are used in architectural practice and they will dictate the type of drawing technique to use. With respect to plans, elevations, and sections, several drawing conventions are possible for the architect to select. Remember that the situation will demand the style or character employed in the delineation of these drawings. If the drawing is to be used as a presentation drawing, then the character might be a style suited for the client's understanding, whereas if the drawing is part of a set of production drawings, then an entirely different method might be used to convey the same information.

Site Plans are a plan view of the site, the building, and the surrounding environment. Often the roof plan will be incorporated with the site plan to help place the building in its proper context. The site plan is normally drawn using the engineer's scale, and the size of the drawing will vary depending upon the size of the project and the sheet size. Typical scales which are used for this drawing are: 1″ = 20′ and 1″ = 30′.

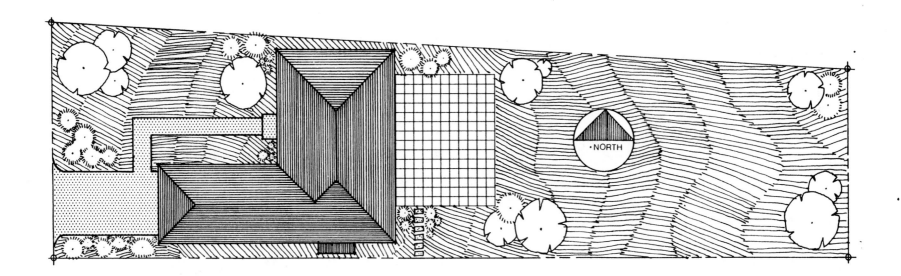

FLOOR PLANS

The Floor Plan is actually a horizontal section placed high enough to locate all windows and doors, and as such is one of the most important drawings since all other drawings must relate to it. The purpose of the floor plan is to show the location of all walls, partitions, and openings. The delineation of the plan will depend upon its intended use and the amount of detail necessary for communication. Thus, the walls could be rendered as a solid, sketched, or drawn to indicate proper building materials and construction.

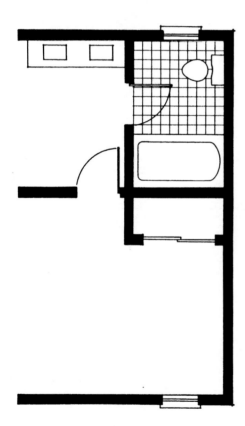
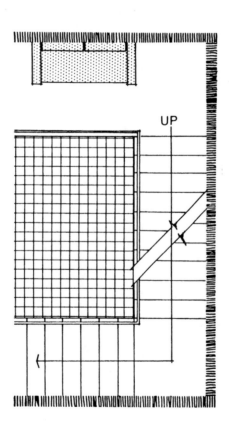
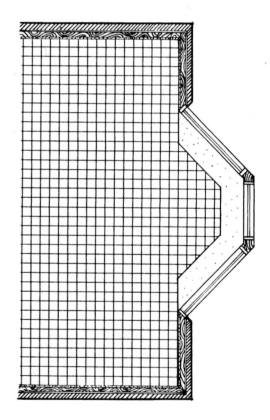

ELEVATIONS

The purpose of the exterior elevation is to show the finished form and appearance of all outside features of the building. This would include all building materials, textures, and window/door fenestrations. Generally most elevations are drawn at the same scale as the floor plans for ease in interpretation. Because elevations are two-dimensional, they can be misleading because certain depth clues are not always evident. Often this problem will be reduced by projecting shades and shadows on the building to provide a sense of depth. Each elevation is labeled with respect to compass directions and is named for the point it faces. Thus the south elevation faces south. Due to the size of some drawings, many elevations are drawn "out of projection" with the plan and placed on a sheet of their own. This is a "conventional violation" with respect to true orthographic projection.

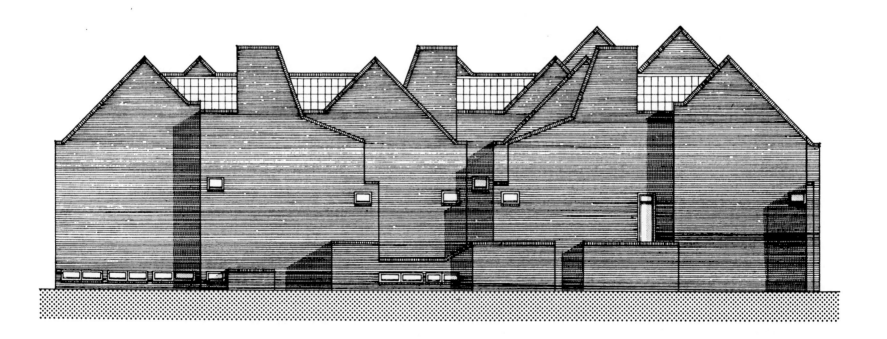

Elevations are valuable in illustrating the form and massing of the structure. The method of delineation will depend upon the drawing use; if intended for presentation to a client, or as part of a set of production drawings. Each situation requires its own drawing language and method of communication. As illustrated below, one should note, that as the size of the drawing increases, more details are shown. The general practice is to draw plans and elevations at 1/8″ or 1/4″ = 1′ − 0″ scales, but other scales can be selected for convenience of size.

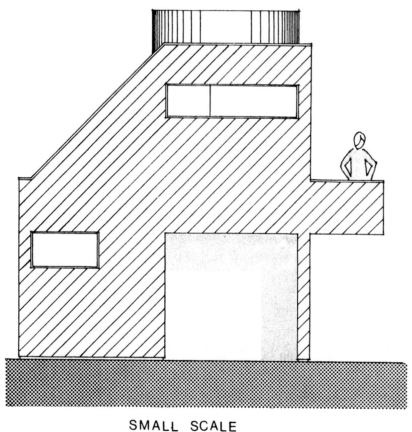

SMALL SCALE

LARGE SCALE

SECTIONS

When using orthographic projection to illustrate an object, the interior details will often be so complex that the finished drawing ends up a maze of hidden lines. Because hidden lines for one part tend to overlap hidden lines from another part, the entire drawing becomes difficult to interpret. To alleviate this problem, various sections are taken to show the interior of an object when it is confusing to use hidden lines. An imaginary cutting-plane is used to "slice" through the building at the designer's discretion allowing the interior to be shown clearly. There are numerous types of sections, all intended to illustrate the object with a minimum amount of hidden lines. Section-lining or cross-hatching is used to indicate building materials at the cut line. The use of these symbols will aid in the visualization of the section and show the building materials being selected.

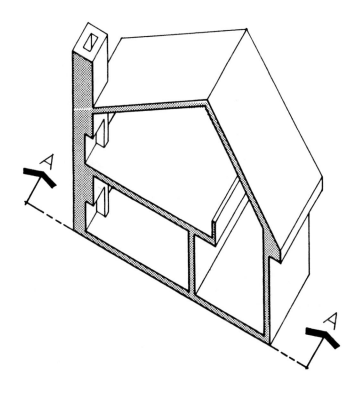

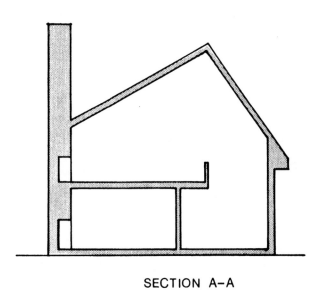

SECTION A–A

SECTIONAL CONVENTIONS

After slicing the object with a cutting-plane, it is standard practice to section line the cut area with an architectural symbol. A variety of symbols have been developed for different materials, many of them standardized within the profession while others may vary with the architectural office or type of work. The use of symbols avoids repetition of information in a more lengthly use of words or notes, and gives an illustration of the cut elements graphically. Some of the more common symbols are given below. Also indicated below are examples of full sections as they would appear in both transverse and longitudinal positions. The offset section should only be used when some distinct advantage is achieved by its use; otherwise it is more difficult to understand than a continuous section.

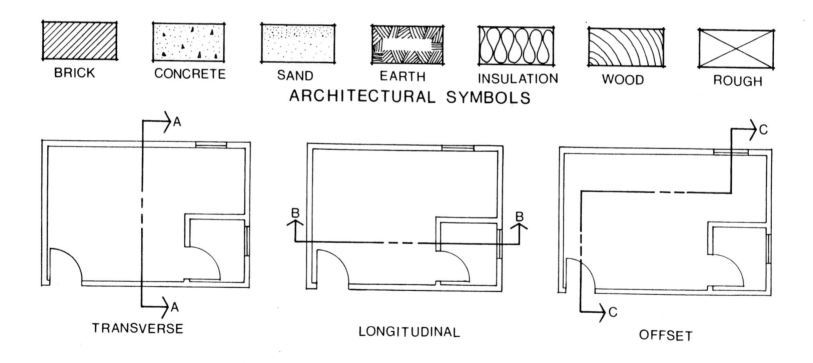

BRICK   CONCRETE   SAND   EARTH   INSULATION   WOOD   ROUGH

ARCHITECTURAL SYMBOLS

TRANSVERSE   LONGITUDINAL   OFFSET

Types of Sections

There are various types of sections used in architectural drawing, with each one selected for its own particular characteristics. When examining a set of production drawings, any number of different types of sections will be encountered. Some of the more standard types are as follows:

1. Full Section — Cuts through the entire object and when taken across the width of the building is called a transverse section. If taken across the length of the building, it is called a longitudinal section.
2. Offset Section — The object is cut by a staggered cutting-plane. This type of section is used when it is not possible to use a continuous cutting-plane.
3. Design Section — Is used to describe the interior of the building; the space occupied by the structure is usually indicated by outlines. The emphasis is on form and definition of the existing spaces.
4. Structural Section — Shows the building construction and on large buildings Detail Sections are taken separately for the various junctions of the building.
5. Half Sections — Are used when the object is symmetrical and when it is desirable to show the inside and the outside in only one view.
6. Partial or Broken-Out Sections — This type of section shows special features without showing an extra view.
7. Revolved Section — Explains the shape of parts to an advantage on symmetrical objects while eliminating the need for an extra view.
8. Detail or Removed Section — Shows the details which are too small to be shown at small scale. Perhaps one of the most widely used sections in a set of production drawings. Used to illustrate details of construction.
9. Conventional Violations are used for the purpose of making it easier to draw and interpret sections.

DESIGN AND STRUCTURAL SECTION

The purpose of a Design Section is to describe the interior space with emphasis on form. The structure is outlined thus making the structural space as inconspicuous as possible. Footings are never shown in design sections.

In a Structural Section the emphasis is on building construction details. Thus the interior design is not indicated and the viewer is left only to consider such elements as footings, walls, floors, and roof junctions. Symbols are used to indicate materials.

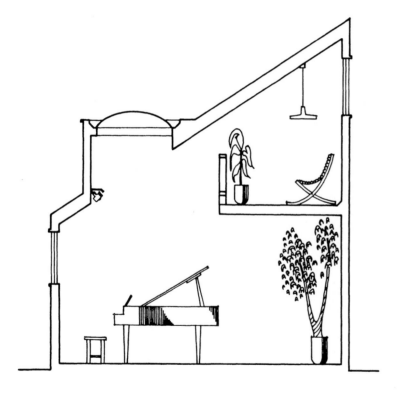

DESIGN SECTION

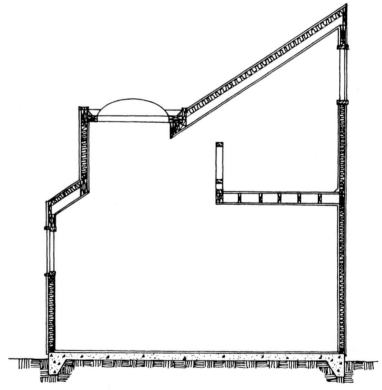

STRUCTURAL SECTION

TYPES OF ARCHITECTURAL SECTIONS

The sections illustrated below are often used in production drawings to communicate details of construction. They are often larger in scale than plans and elevations and therefore more detailed graphically. As a rule, most detail drawings are prepared at the smallest scale practical. This may be anywhere from 1/4″ = 1′-0″ up to 3″ = 1′-0″.

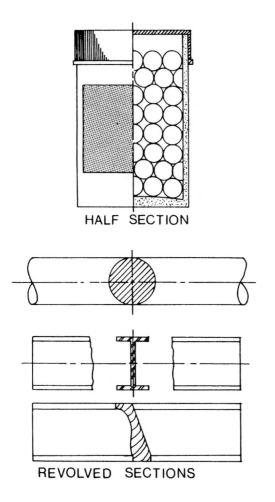

HALF SECTION

REVOLVED SECTIONS

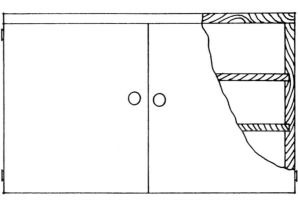

PARTIAL OR BROKEN-OUT SECTION

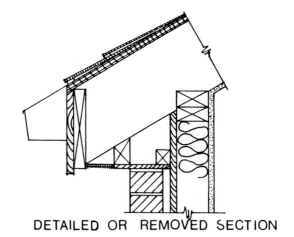

DETAILED OR REMOVED SECTION

DETAILED OR REMOVED SECTION

If the front elevation of the window is not drawn at a large enough scale to make revolved sections practical then detailed sections are the appropriate choice. In the illustration shown below, detail sections A-A and B-B are drawn removed and at a larger scale in order to illustrate the profile of the window sash. Often detail sections of this type will be drawn without showing the cutting plane position.

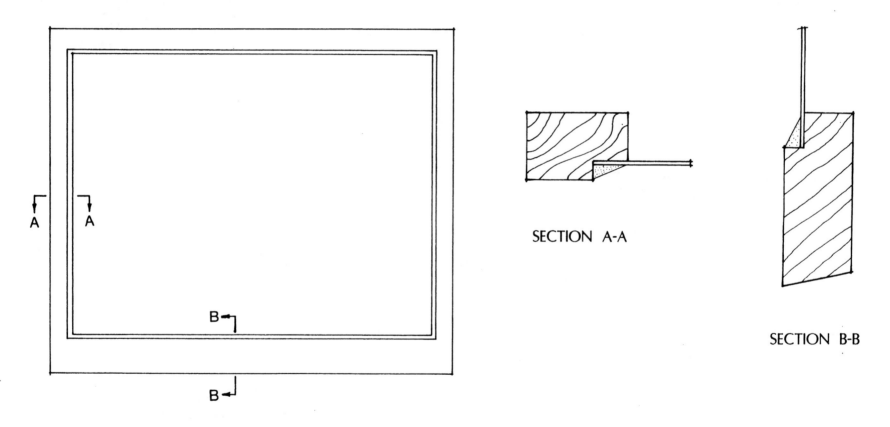

SECTION A-A

SECTION B-B

ELEVATION OF WINDOW

CONVENTIONAL PRACTICES AND VIOLATIONS

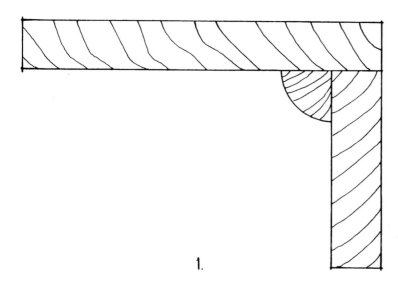

1.

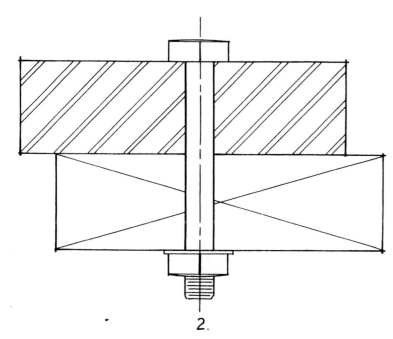

2.

Section lines are used to illustrate where a part has been cut and also helps the architect to communicate the type of material being used by the appropriate use of building symbol. When two sectioned parts are next to each other, as shown in example 1, it is customary to crosshatch them in different directions for clarity. Otherwise the observer might think the part is made from one piece rather than three separate pieces. Another procedure that has been adopted in standard architectural practice is termed a ``conventional violation of projection''. For example, it is a conventional practice not to section bolts, screws, rivets, handles, etc. when in section. The criteria being: these parts are better explained when they are not sectioned. Thus in examples 2 and 3 the bolt and handle are not section lined even though the cutting plane would pass through them and in conventional theory they would be sectioned. This practice is normally followed in most cases in order to clarify the drawings and not make them too cluttered with crosshatching.

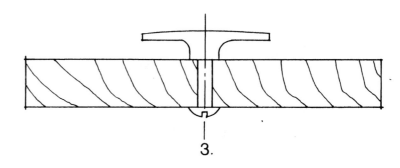

3.

TYPICAL WALL SECTIONS

Another very useful section is the typical wall section. This is generally a full vertical section which shows the building construction throughout the majority of the structure. It is especially useful when a building has few exceptions in its method of construction. The section is not taken at any particular place in plan, but is typical for most of the building. Depending upon the size and complexity of the building, it is possible to have typical wall sections illustrating several different wall conditions.

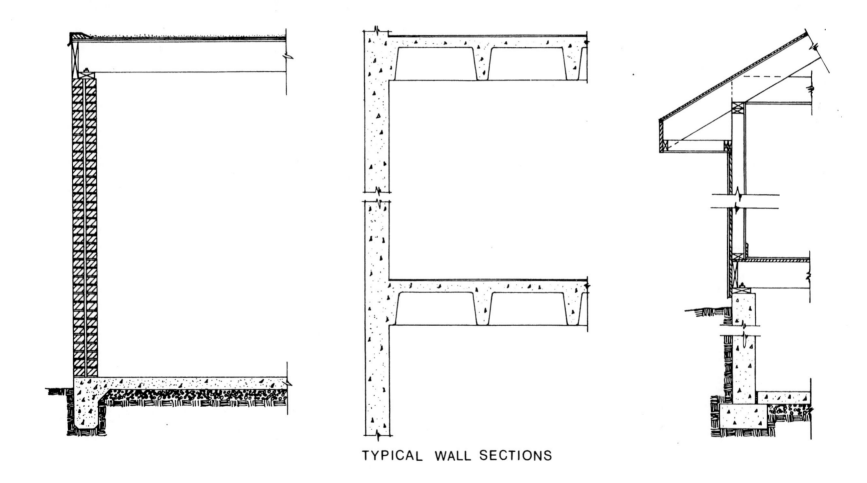

TYPICAL WALL SECTIONS

TYPICAL WALL SECTIONS

Show below are two typical wall sections of wood frame construction that have been dimensioned and labeled. In one case all of the labeling has been organized flush left which allows for the vertical dimensions to be placed to the right of the section. In the second example, the labeling of building materials has been integrated into the entire drawing which results in a cleaner less crowded drawing.

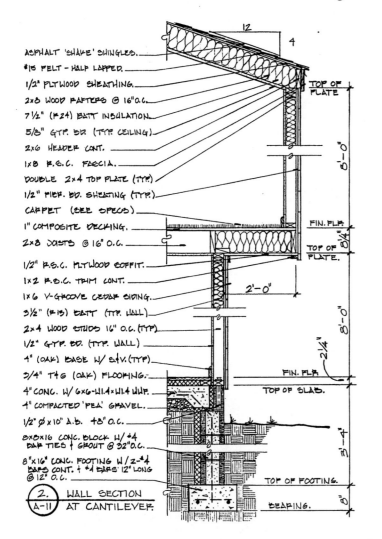

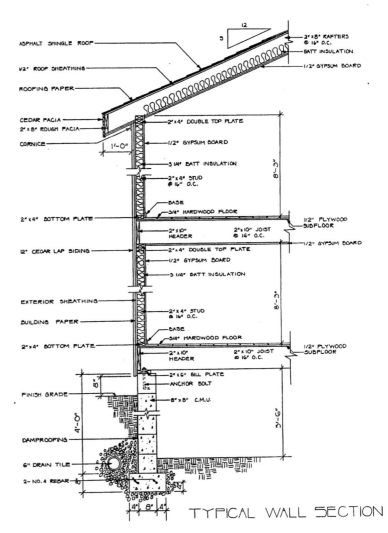

BUILDING SECTIONS

The building section is an example of a full section. In the cases shown below each section is taken across the short dimension of the plan so that they are also transverse sections. The amount of detail which is shown in each section is left up to the discretion of the designer. The circles on the drawings refer to the location of details which can be found on the sheets noted by the fraction. For example, if the detail circle indicates a fraction as 3/A11, this means that the drawing for this situation is located on sheet A11 and is detail number 3 on that sheet.

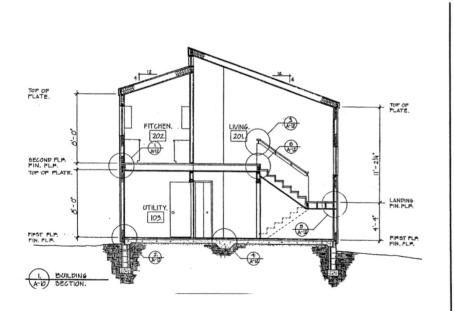

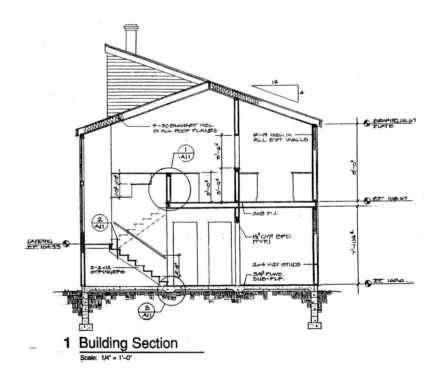

1 Building Section

Scale: 1/4" = 1'-0"

Dimensioning

Dimensioning practices vary within the different professions, such as building construction and land measurement. Each particular occupation will have its own standards and methods of dimensioning practices. The dimensions necessary for any production drawing are simply those necessary for constructing the building. This means the dimensions will be based on the actual procedure in constructing the building as well as those dimensions necessary for determining size and location requirements. Dimensions are placed on plans, elevations, sections, and details, and will be read as either horizontal (plans) or vertical (elevations). The number of dimensions will depend upon the complexity of the building and the nature of the individual drawing.

Dimensions on plans are composed of two types, either overall or intermediate. The overall dimensions give the largest height, width, and depth whereas intermediate give the size and location of architectural elements. Overall dimensions are placed outside the drawing using dimension and extension lines. Intermediate dimensions are placed on the inside of the overall dimensions so that they act as a continuous chain and provide a running total. Such a procedure is considered a convention of architectural dimensioning. Other conventions are:

1. Neatness, legibility, size of letters and numerals, spacing the dimension lines to avoid crowding, placing the dimensions nearest the part for which it is describing, keeping dimensions off the interior part of the drawing to allow notes, and any other rules that could be made concerning the placement of dimensions, are all prompted by the consideration to make the drawings easy to read and pleasing in appearance.
2. Numerals are placed above the dimension line and all dimension lines are terminated by arrowheads.
3. The use of the foot marks (') and inch marks (") varies in practice.
4. Dimensions are so aligned that they read from either the bottom or right side of all drawings.

As previously stated, many dimensions in architecture are based on the actual procedure in constructing the building. For example, the difference in locating doors, windows, and partitions in masonry and wood frame construction will vary. In masonry construction the dimensions for the masonry openings of doors and windows are needed while the wall is being constructed, but in frame construction the entire stud wall is erected before any openings are located. In locating partitions, the masonry wall is dimensioned to its face while the frame partition is located to the stud wall. Details of construction showing the thickness of each wall type can best be shown at a larger scale in a detailed drawing.

The overall dimensions on frame construction are given to the outside of the stud frame wall because that dimension is used first, before the sheathing and other wall materials are applied. Even in masonry veneer on wood frame, the overall dimension is to the stud frame because the frame is constructed before the brick is placed. An overall dimension including the veneer would indicate how much space the building would occupy but would not be a dimension necessary for construction, except on the foundation plan which would then show how the veneer is supported.

Large scale drawings are usually either sectional detail drawings of the plan or vertical sections showing the construction of walls, floors, ceilings, or roofs and their intersection. Vertical sectional details are often more involved and essential to the illustration of the construction and design than plan sectional drawings. It is vital that levels of major elements such as floors and roofs be dimensioned with elevational mark symbols and that all dimensions correlate properly between sections so that they complement the principal drawings. Typical large scale detail drawings would include roof-wall sections, floor-wall sections, roof, wall and floor sections, wall plan sections, stair details, door details, window details, and cabinetry details.

Masonry and Wood Frame Dimensioning

Illustrated below are masonry and wood frame floor plans dimensioned according to accepted architectural conventions. Note, either arrowheads or slash marks can be used on dimensional lines. If dots are used, they indicate modular dimensioning.

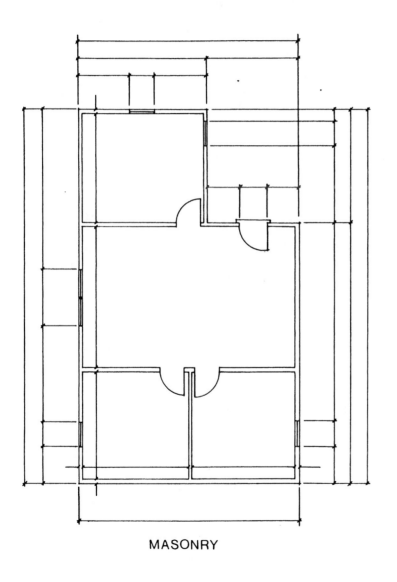

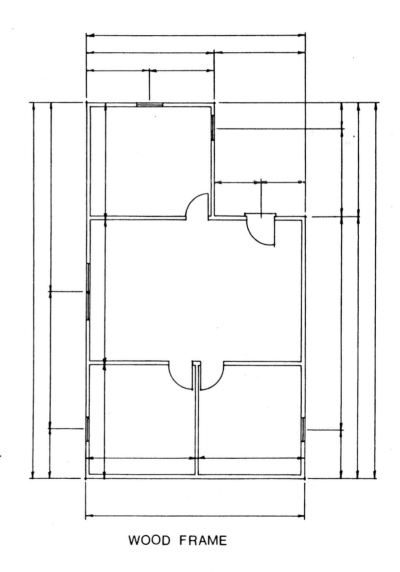

MASONRY   WOOD FRAME

DIMENSIONING PRACTICES

Two large scale drawings with proper dimensioning practices.

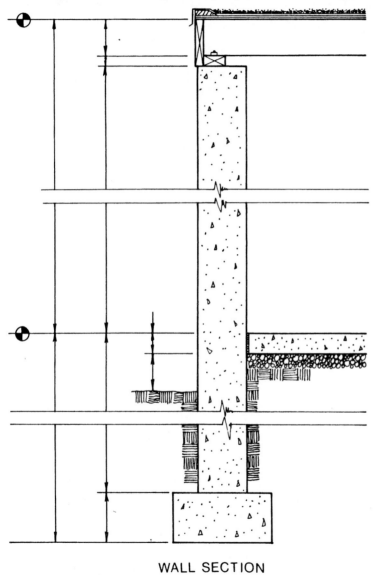

WALL SECTION

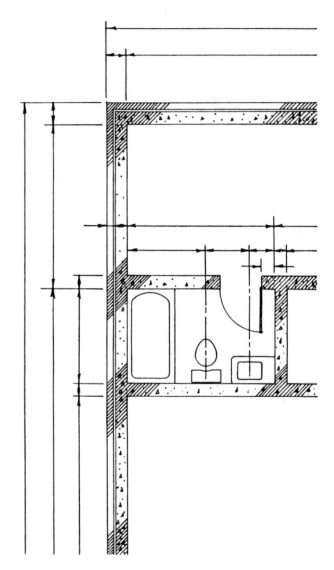

PARTIAL FLOOR PLAN

CHAPTER 7

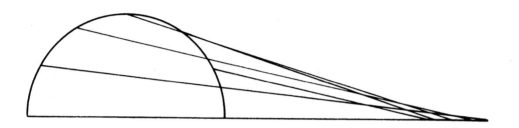

GEOMETRY IN ARCHITECTURE

GEOMETRY IN ARCHITECTURE

Geometry in architecture as it applies in this context, is concerned with surfaces and solids which are often used in the profession. The following examples of lines, surfaces, and solids are those which are most commonly found in geometry. In order to understand how each surface or solid is generated, the following definitions are given:

1. A Generatrix is a curved or straight line, the path of which generates a surface.
2. The path of the generatrix is controlled by a Plane Director.
3. A Single-Curved surface has straight line elements which can be developed into a plane or rolled out.
4. A Double-Curved surface is generated by the motion of a curved line.
5. A Warped surface is generated by consecutive straight line elements which are non-parallel and non-intersecting.
6. A Ruled surface is generated by the path of a straight or curved line.

The various classification of surfaces and solids are shown below.

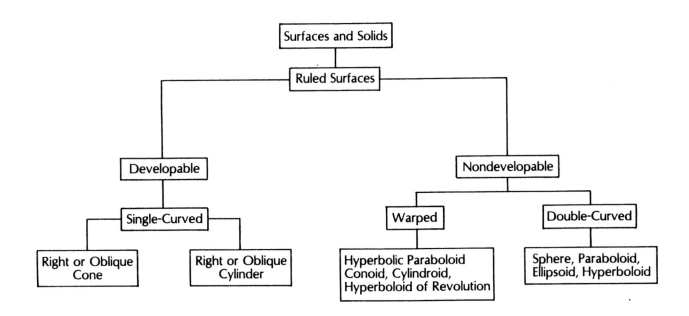

Illustrated below are some of the more common curved lines used in architecture.

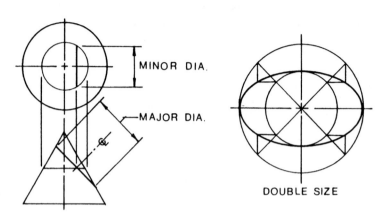

ELLIPSE

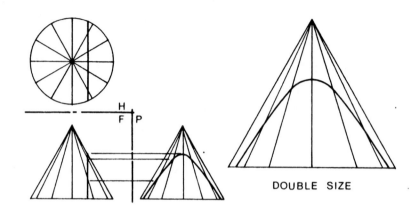

HYPERBOLA

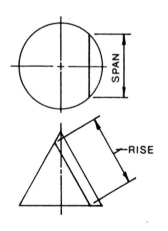

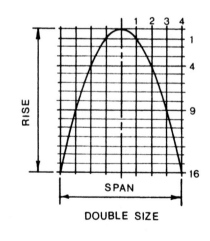

PARABOLA

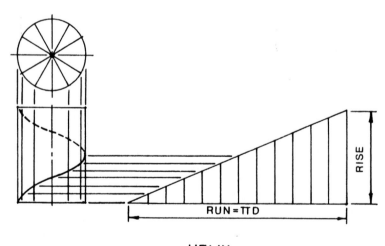

HELIX

SINGLE-CURVED SURFACES

Single-Curved surfaces of cones and cylinders are generated by a straight line whose successive positions are either parallel or intersecting. These surfaces are capable of being developed or rolled out into a pattern.

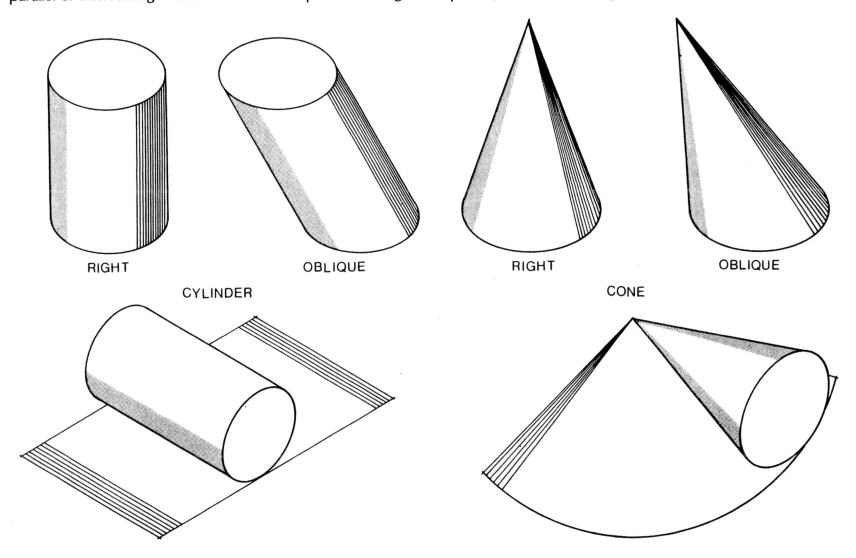

RIGHT   OBLIQUE   RIGHT   OBLIQUE

CYLINDER   CONE

WARPED SURFACES

A warped surface is a ruled surface on which the consecutive elements are skew to each other. A variety of warped surfaces which can be found in architecture are illustrated below.

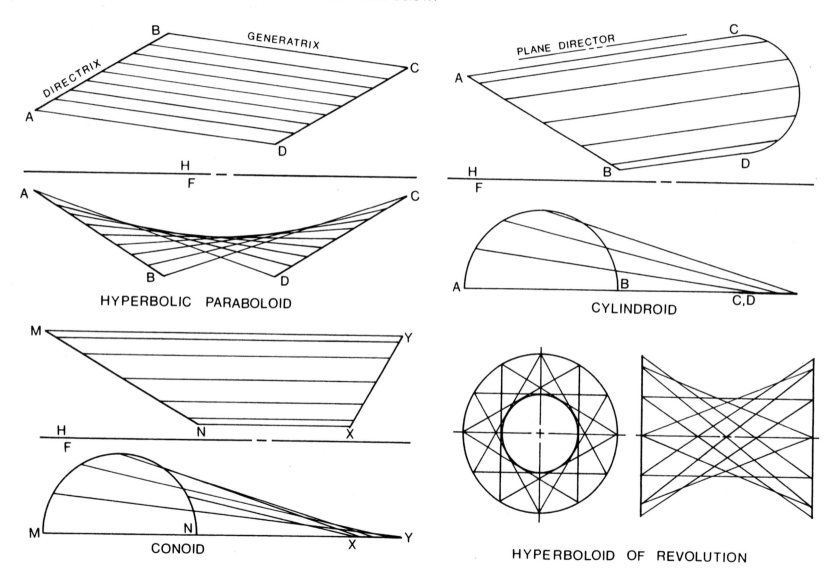

HYPERBOLIC PARABOLOID

CYLINDROID

CONOID

HYPERBOLOID OF REVOLUTION

DOUBLE-CURVED SURFACES

A double-curved surface is generated by the motion of a curved line. Four of these surfaces are described and shown below.

1. Sphere: A circle is revolved about its diameter.
2. Prolate Ellipsoid: An ellipse is revolved about its major axis.
3. Paraboloid: A parabolic curve is rotated about its principal axis.
4. Hyperboloid: A hyperbolic curve is rotated about its principal axis.

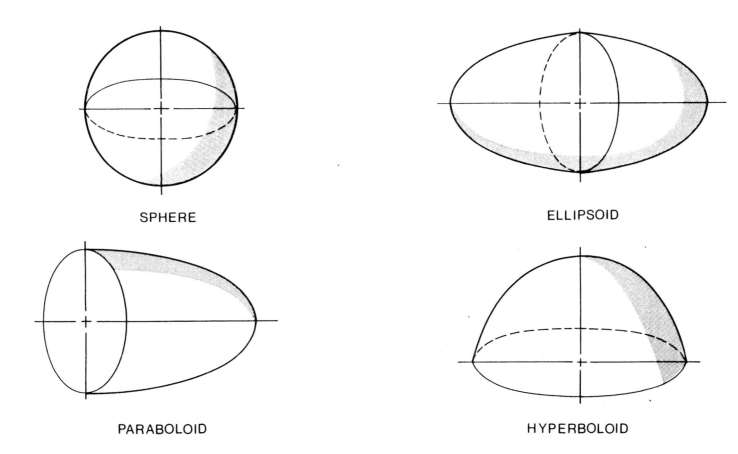

SPHERE

ELLIPSOID

PARABOLOID

HYPERBOLOID

DEVELOPMENT OF SURFACES

Often surfaces of solids can be developed or "rolled out" into a pattern. A prime example of this are those solids bounded by plane or single-curved surfaces. All surfaces can be developed approximately and many can be developed exactly. Those which can be developed exactly are the prism, cylinder, right cone, and pyramid while the oblique pyramid, oblique cone, and sphere are surfaces which can only be developed through approximation. The amount of error in the approximate developments can be reduced by dividing the surface into a number of small elements. Illustrated on the next two pages are examples of developments of plane and single-curved surfaces.

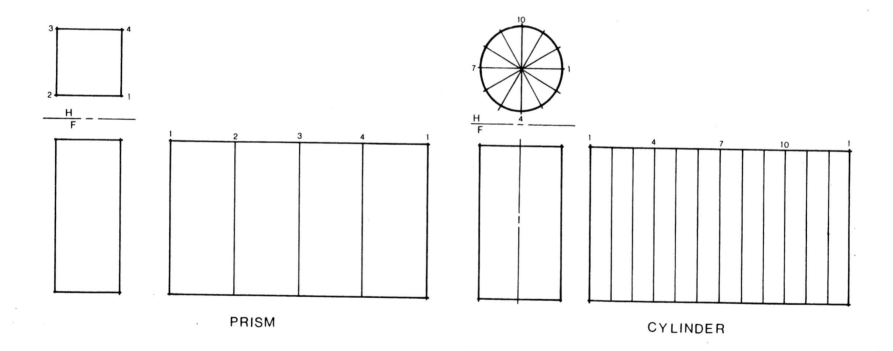

PRISM

CYLINDER

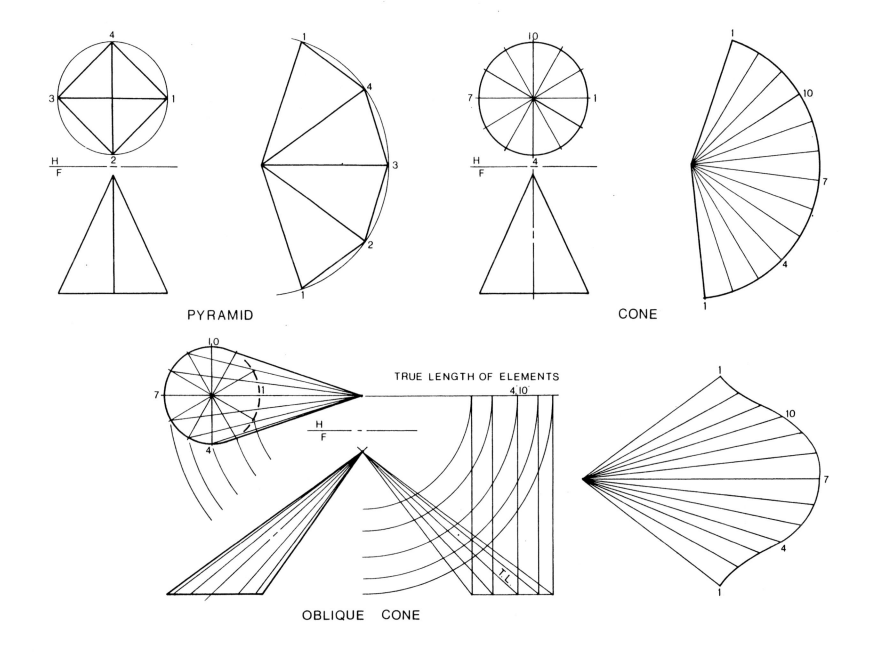

PYRAMID

CONE

TRUE LENGTH OF ELEMENTS

OBLIQUE CONE

INTERSECTION OF SOLIDS

Determining the line of intersection between different types of solids or surfaces has great practical application in architecture. Virtually all buildings have a multitude of intersection problems which must be resolved in some manner. Many are worked out on the job, whereas the larger problems like roof surface intersections are solved at some point in the design stage. Most intersections of ruled surfaces can be achieved either by the use of cutting-planes or the piercing point method where one of the views shows the involved planes as edges. The cutting-plane method is suggested for use when single-curved surfaces are involved. The principle to remember when using cutting-planes is to pass them so that cut elements are easily identified and drawn, such as circles or straight lines. Elements such as an ellipse, parabola or hyperbola take time to draw and identify. The illustrations on this page show the use of cutting-planes on a variety of solids and the resultant lines of intersections.

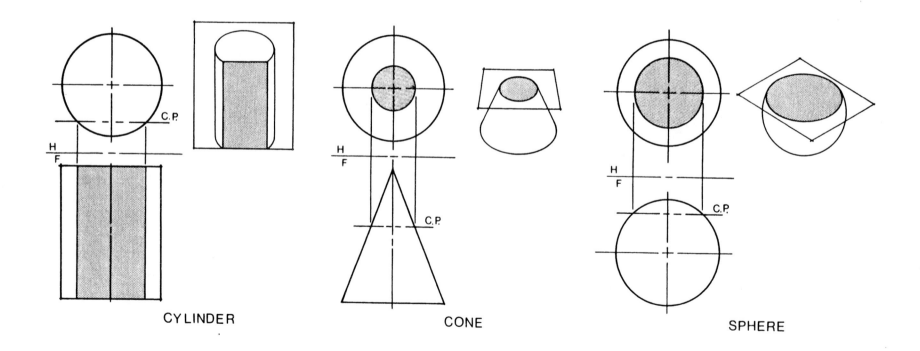

CYLINDER   CONE   SPHERE

The illustrations on this page show the use of vertical and horizontal cutting-planes to find the line of intersection between solids.

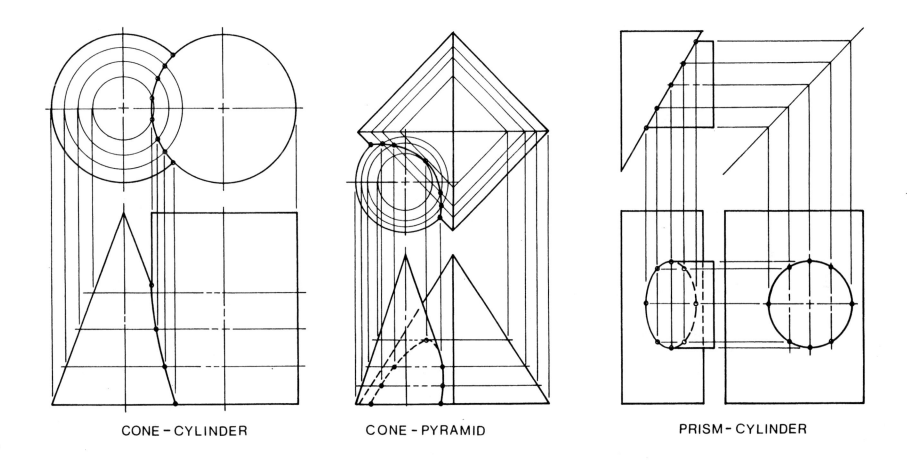

CONE - CYLINDER   CONE - PYRAMID   PRISM - CYLINDER

CHAPTER **8**

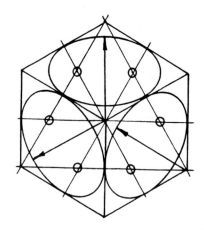

PICTORIAL DRAWING—AXONOMETRIC AND OBLIQUE

Pictorial Drawing

Pictorial drawings are used when it is desirable to show three dimensions of height, width, and length in one single drawing. Because it is easier to visualize an object when these principal dimensions are illustrated, pictorial drawings are especially suited to architecture. The term "pictorial drawing" refers to all types of drawings which show three dimensions in a single view. More specifically, the types of pictorial drawings can be classified into: Axonometric, Oblique, and Perspective. The choice of a particular type depends upon a number of considerations: the choice of view desired, the amount of realism necessary, and the amount of time available for construction. As will be seen, some types of pictorials are very realistic in their illustration of a building, whereas other types can be very diagrammatic and present the building in an idealized or technical manner.

Axonometric is a type of pictorial which is derived through the system of orthographic projection and includes the following: Isometric, Dimetric, and Trimetric. The specific type depends upon how the object is turned or tilted to emphasize certain sides. In isometric, the object is turned in such a position that all sides appear equal. If a cube is used as an example, it is tilted so that its diagonal is seen as a point. Thus when drawn in this manner all sides will have equal emphasis because the three principal axes are all at equal angles with respect to each other. Given any two related views of an object, it is possible to draw an axonometric of the object using the system of orthographic projection. This usually requires drawing two auxiliary views before the final drawing is achieved. It is a customary procedure, in the interest of time and convenience, to construct axonometric drawings directly without projections. When this approach is taken, it is called an axonometric drawing as opposed to an axonometric projection. The drawing will be slightly larger than the true projections when this method is used, but valuable drawing time is saved if the proper angles and scale ratios are known for each type of axonometric selected. Thus most pictorials of the axonometric type are constructed as drawings rather than projections.

Isometric and Dimetric Theory

Below are examples of isometric and diametric projections, and for comparison purposes, the object as it would appear as a drawing. Trimetric is derived similarly to isometric/dimetric but differs in that no two faces receive equal emphasis. The scales and angles become more involved, to a point where perspective would be a better choice.

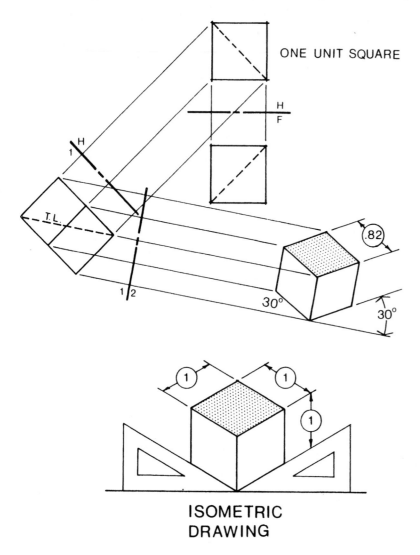

ISOMETRIC DRAWING

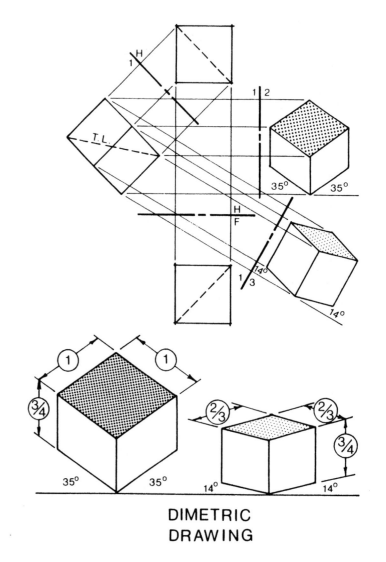

DIMETRIC DRAWING

ISOMETRIC DRAWING — POSITION OF AXES

As derived in the isometric projection example illustrated earlier, the axes in isometric are at 120 degrees to each other. This equal sided relationship makes it possible to arrange the axes in isometric drawings in three different positions. The normal position looks down on the object while the reversed position looks up from the bottom. The horizontal position is best suited for objects having one principal dimension greater than the other two. The three drawings shown below illustrate these possibilities.

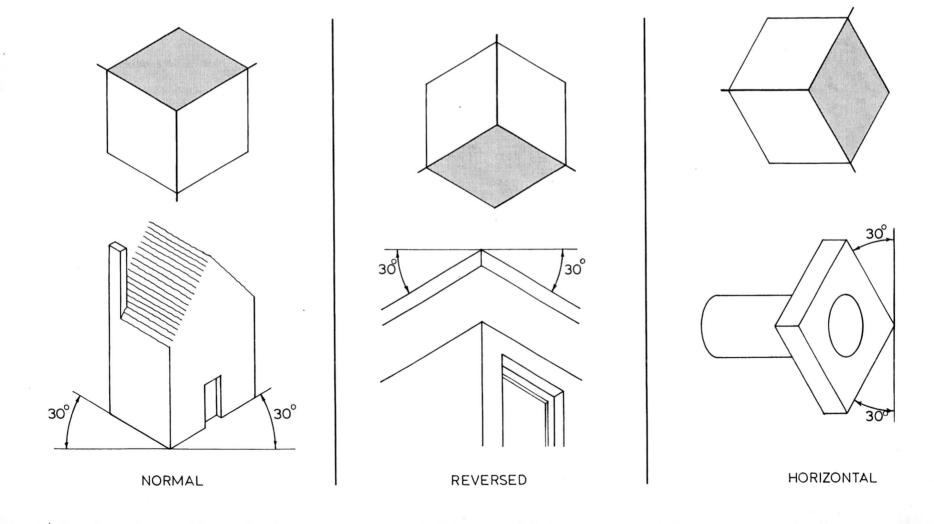

NORMAL   REVERSED   HORIZONTAL

ISOMETRIC DRAWING — NON-ISOMETRIC LINES

When constructing an isometric drawing lines which are not parallel to the axes are called non-isometric lines. As such they must be plotted using their end points even if their true lengths are known. This takes place because only lines which make angles of 30 degrees along the right and left axes and vertical lines are in true length in the pictorial if the normal and reversed positions of the axes are used. In the drawings shown below each object is composed of some non-isometric lines. For example, the base of the pyramid can be constructed in isometric because it is basically a rectangle. To find its apex or peak, its top point must be located and the sides then drawn to the base. The sides of the pyramid are considered non-isometric lines.

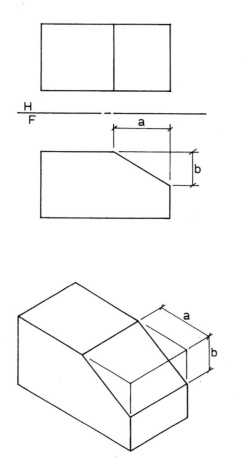

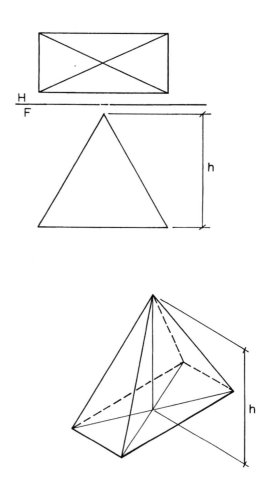

ISOMETRIC DRAWING — FOUR-CENTERED ELLIPSE

Circles and arcs can be drawn in isometric but must be constructed to appear elliptical. One method for constructing a circle in isometric is drawing a four-centered ellipse. An ellipse is constructed using four center points from which four arcs are drawn which when connected form the ellipse. The construction is as follows:

1. An isometric parallelogram is constructed which is equal to the diameter of the proposed circle. Centerlines are located on each side.
2. Diagonals are constructed from points a, b, c, and d to the opposite sides. Where the diagonals cross locates two of the centers.
3. These two centers are used to scribe the small radius which forms the ends of the ellipse.
4. Complete the ellipse by drawing large arcs from each corner as illustrated. In the final drawing, all arcs should match evenly to form a smooth curve and the ellipse which is the circle in isometric.

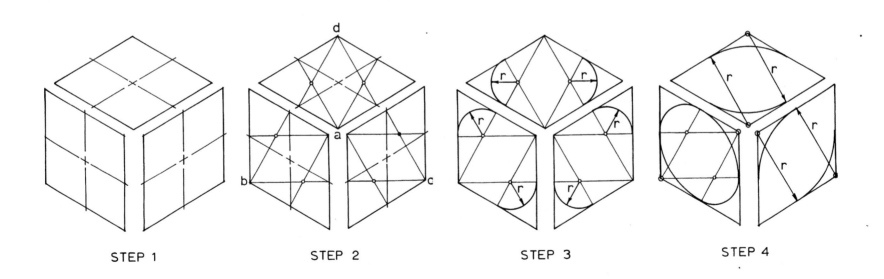

STEP 1   STEP 2   STEP 3   STEP 4

ISOMETRIC DRAWING

The layout of an isometric drawing is illustrated in the example shown below. The orthographic drawings are assumed to be the given information with the resultant pictorial of the house drawn in isometric.

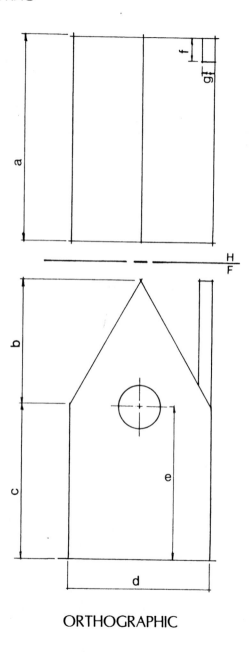

ORTHOGRAPHIC

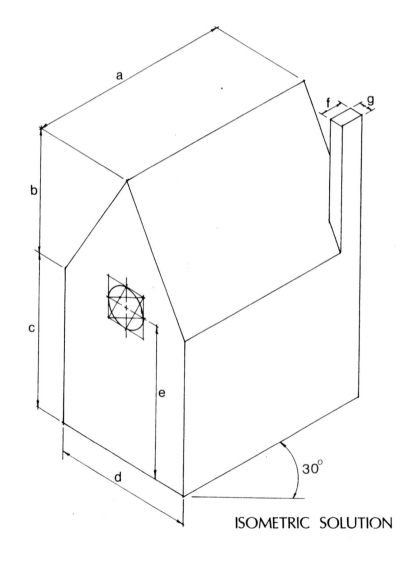

ISOMETRIC SOLUTION

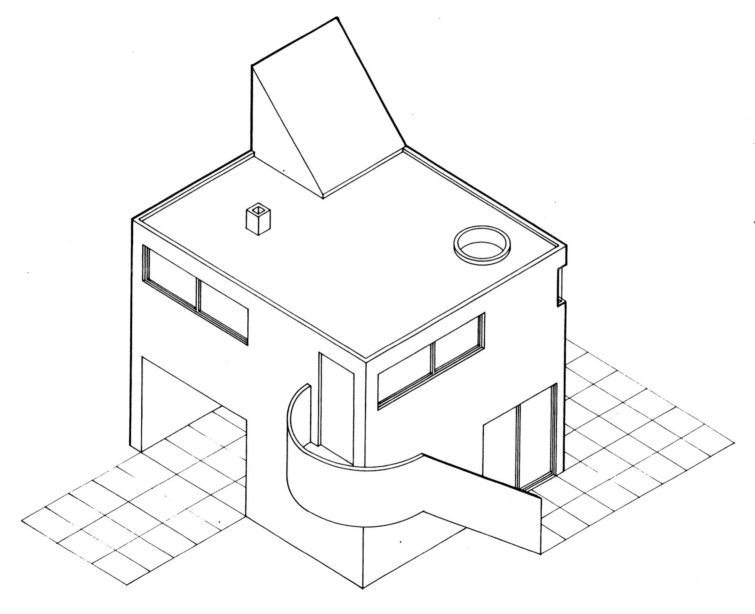

ISOMETRIC

DIMETRIC DRAWING

In dimetric drawing, two of the three principal axes are foreshortened equally leaving the third unequal. By using appropriate angles and proportional scales, it is possible to allow for this condition. Thus two scales and various combinations of angles are used and while it might take longer to draw than isometric, it is often more desirable because one of the faces can be emphasized or subordinated to better suit the purpose of the drawing. The numbers indicate the scale ratios to be used for each axis. The angles approximate those derived from orthorgraphic projection.

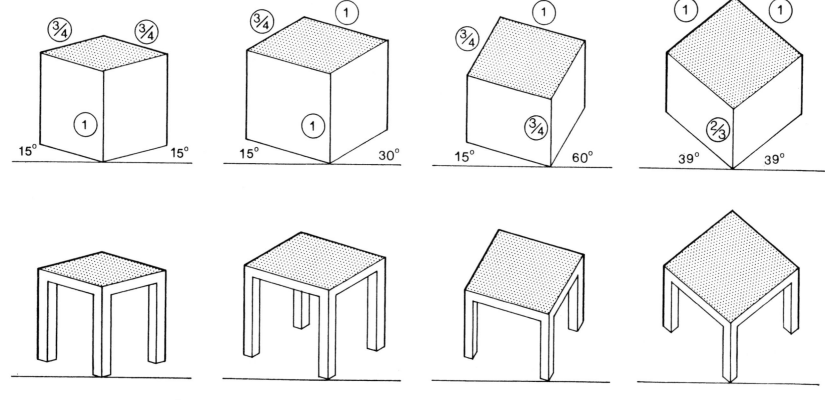

DIMETRIC

DIMETRIC DRAWING — ADDITIONAL POSITIONS OF THE AXES

The preceding page illustrates four positions of the axes in dimetric which are often used for developing architectural pictorials. Since one of the possible dimetric pictorial places the axes such that the object is turned so that two of its axes make the same angle and the third axis makes a different angle the drawing angles appear symmetrical. Likewise it is possible to obtain a view in which the axes appear unsymmetrical. Examples of these types along with their scale ratios are shown below.

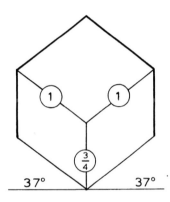 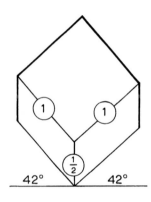 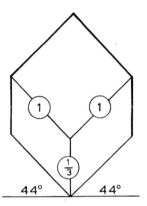 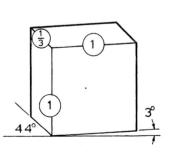

SYMMETRICAL

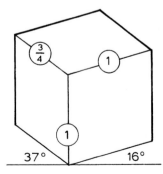 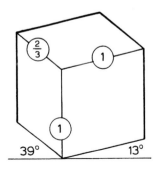 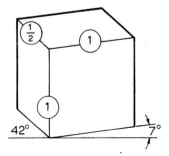

UNSYMMETRICAL

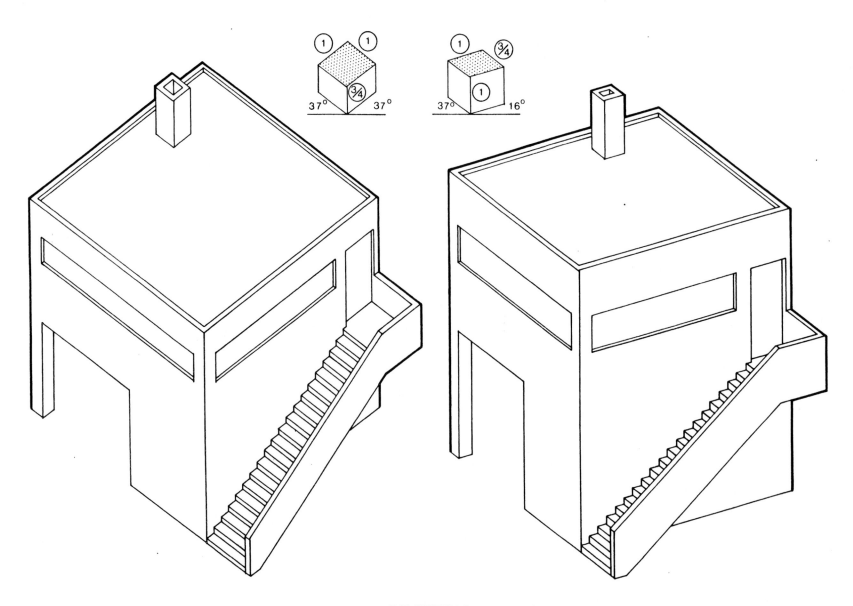

DIMETRIC

SECTIONAL AXONOMETRIC

Sectional pictorial is a very useful method for illustrating how the various component parts relate to each other.

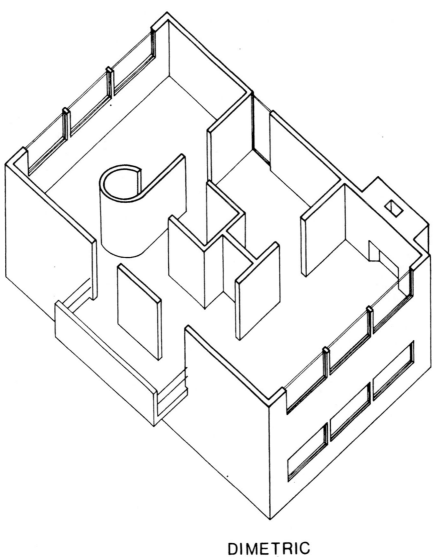

DIMETRIC

OBLIQUE DRAWING

Oblique projection uses parallel projectors, not perpendicular to the picture plane but oblique to it, thereby making it possible to see three faces of a rectangular object in one pictorial view when the front face of the object is parallel to the picture plane as in multi-view orthographic. Because the front face is parallel to the picture plane it will be exactly the same as the front view in orthographic and will show it in true size and shape. Thus oblique drawings are often used in architectural drawing as either elevational oblique or plan oblique. Another quality of oblique drawing is that circles and arcs can be drawn with a compass if they are on or parallel to the front face of projection.

The different types of oblique drawings are determined by the depth of the receding axis and are classified as: Cavalier, General, and Cabinet. Cavalier is quickest to draw because it uses only one scale but has the most distortion. General is probably the best looking for its proportions but has awkard receding scales, while cabinet is most widely accepted because it is easy to draw and is a good compromise between the other two types.

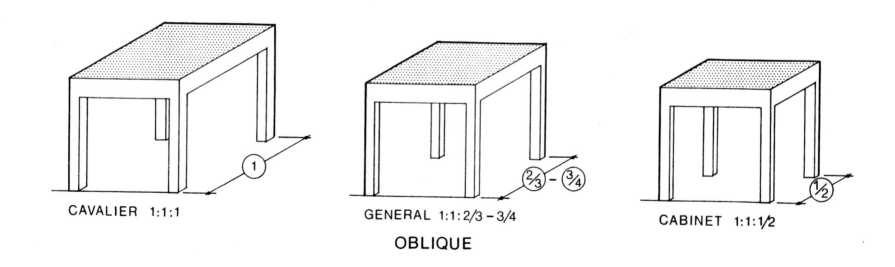

CAVALIER 1:1:1   GENERAL 1:1:2/3 − 3/4   CABINET 1:1:1/2

OBLIQUE

ELEVATIONAL OBLIQUE

Elevational obliques are often used to give a quick impression of the form and spatial quality of a building and as such often appear diagrammatic and technical. Because the front face is parallel to the picture plane it will appear in true size and shape thus allowing for the illustration of considerable detail in this plane. The angle of the receding axis is any convenient angle such as 30°, 45°, or 60° or any other appropriate angle and the depth of the drawing will be determined by its classification of either cavalier, general, or cabinet.

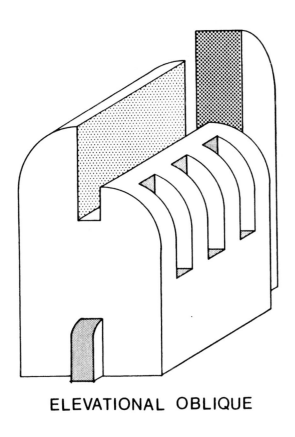

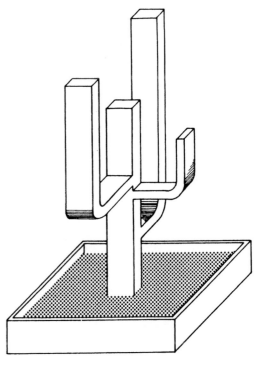

ELEVATIONAL OBLIQUE   ELEVATIONAL OBLIQUE

PLAN OBLIQUES

Using plan oblique pictorial is actually the same as the General Oblique Drawing, only the plan is turned to make the true shape face appear as the top or plan. Using this method, if a plan or a layout of a building is available, it can simply be traced and the third vertical dimension easily added to make it a pictorial. In the illustrations shown below only the plans are given and the heights (h) are assumed and measured using General Oblique scales of 2/3 to 3/4 of the actual height. This method is versatile in its application because the plan is drawn using full 1:1 scale ratios and circles and arcs are drawn with one center with a compass.

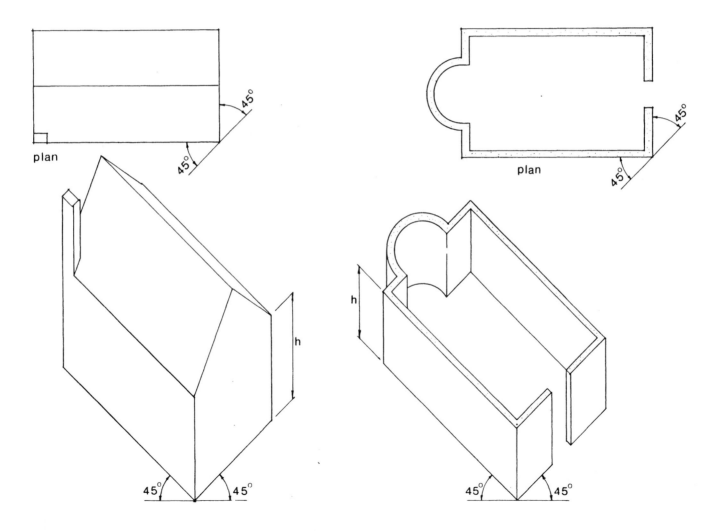

PLAN OBLIQUES

Plan obliques allow for the observer to see the building looking down on either the total building mass or a sectional portion of the building such as an individual level or floor. This type of pictorial is very effective in architectural communication because it allows for quick visualization and comprehension of concepts. One has only to rotate the plan to its proper position and then decide upon the type of oblique drawing to use.

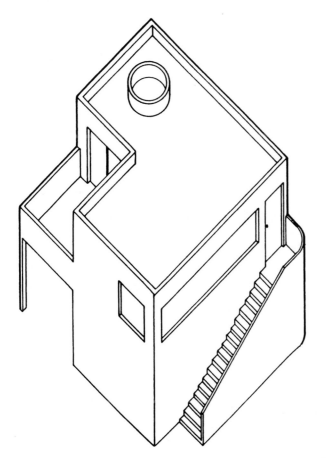
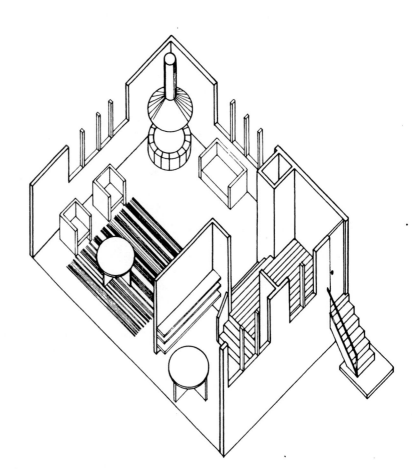

PLAN OBLIQUE

Plan Oblique

Often plan oblique techniques can be used on a floor plan to indicate shadows. The actual length of the shadow is predetermined and is used on those elements that help the plan to "read." In the case of the plan illustrated on this page, the shadows are used to give a better impression of the space being presented.

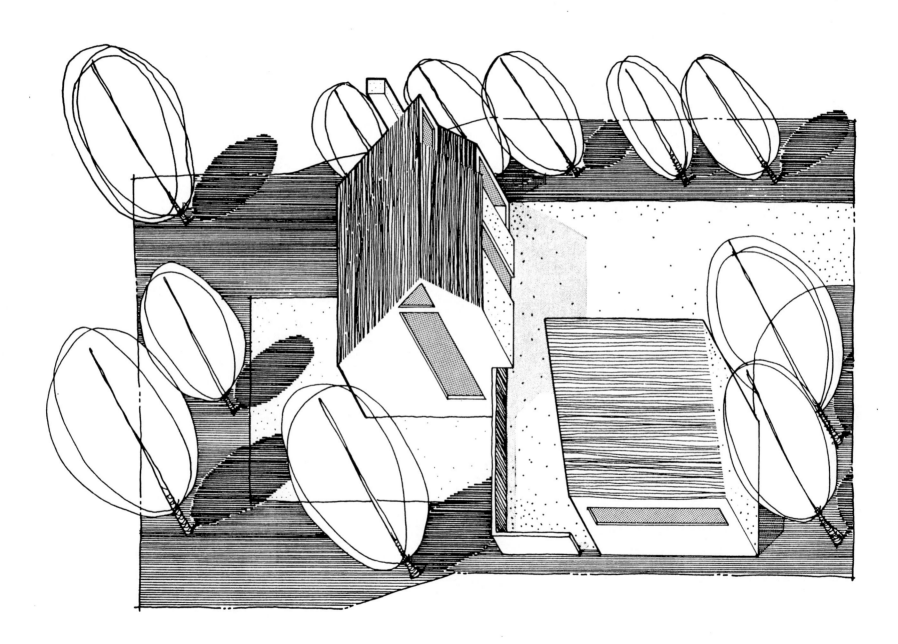

CHAPTER 9

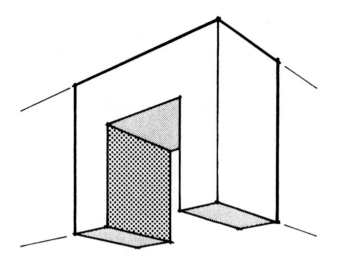

PERSPECTIVE

PERSPECTIVE DRAWING

Perspective is a type of pictorial drawing which gives the most natural appearance of any type of drawing. It represents the reality of a building as one would naturally perceive it. In multi-view projection, the projectors are perpendicular to the plane of projection; thus only two dimensions are represented in any given view. These dimensions are full size regardless of the distance the object is placed away from the picture plane and no convergence is evident. In perspective, there is convergence and it is this characteristic which distinguishes it from multi-view drawing. Other distinguishing characteristics of perspective are the foreshortening effect of lines and planes as they approach horizontal and the decreasing illusion of equal sized objects as they diminish in perspective.

The comparison is often made between the theory of perspective and the results achieved by the use of a camera. Both are very similar in theory but a camera is capable of only producing a perspective picture of a real object, while perspective drawing provides an image not only of objects in existence, but also of ideas and concepts which do not yet exist and are in the conceptual phase. Thus perspective drawing is a very important aspect of design and architecture because it has many uses throughout the entire design process.

It is important to recognize that a perspective drawing has the same basic geometric relationships as the given object itself. These geometrical relationships are controlled by the relationships which exist between the following three elements: the object, the picture plane, and the sight point. The position and placement of these three elements will determine the type of perspective, the angle of view, and the amount of allowable distortion. Thus it is important to immediately determine how these elements can influence the resultant perspective.

PERSPECTIVE NOMENCLATURE

The following perspective nomenclature is used to describe important perspective terms:

SIGHT POINT (SP): Is the location and position of the observer and is the point from which visual rays or lines radiate to the object through the picture plane.

CONE OF VISION (CV): Is the maximum angle of vision which is allowed for the perspective without causing a great degree of distortion.

PICTURE PLANE (PP): Is the imaginary plane which is perpendicular to the observer's line of sight on which the perspective is outlined.

GROUND PLANE (GP): Is the horizontal reference plane which allows the sight point and object to be located vertically.

GROUND LINE (GL): Is the line of intersection between the picture plane and the ground plane. It is used as a reference plane for taking vertical measurements.

HORIZON LINE (HL): Is the line of intersection formed by passing a level plane through the sight point and the picture plane. It is located at the same height as the eye of the observer.

VANISHING POINT (VP): Is the point at the limit of vision where parallel lines appear to converge. Each family or set of parallel lines has its own vanishing point. If the family of parallel lines are horizontal, they will appear to intersect on the horizon line. If the family of lines slope downward from the observer then the vanishing points will be below the horizon line; and if the family of lines slope upward from the observer then the vanishing points will be located above the horizon line. Any given perspective drawing may contain any number of vanishing points due to the large number of possible families of parallel lines. Most perspectives are classified by the number of major vanishing points used.

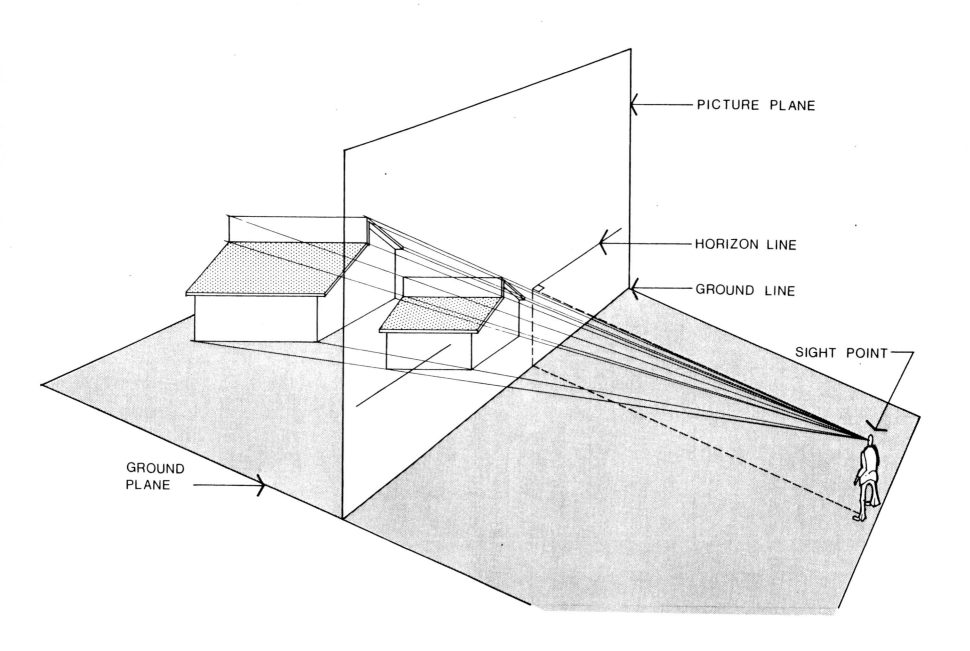

PICTURE PLANE

HORIZON LINE

GROUND LINE

SIGHT POINT

GROUND
PLANE

PERSPECTIVE TYPES

The type of perspective is influenced by the observer's point of view and the orientation of the object with respect to the picture plane. In architecture, the three most common types of perspective are:

1. One-point or parallel perspective, occurs when one of the three principal planes of the object is parallel to the picture plane and for this reason is similar oblique projection.

2. Two-point, or angular perspective, occurs when two of the principal planes of the object are oblique to the picture plane which allows for two sets of vanishing points. This gives a more natural view of the object.

3. Three-point perspective requires separate vanishing points for each of the three principal planes of the object. It is the most natural looking of the three types, but is the least used because the degree of complexity does not warrant the effort for most architectural situations.

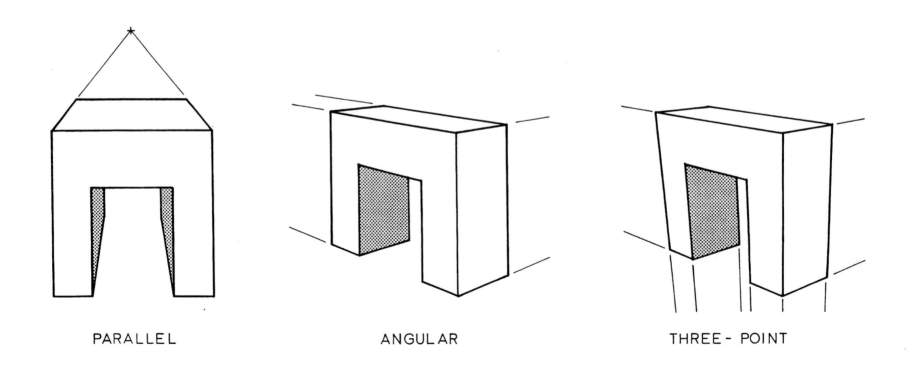

PARALLEL   ANGULAR   THREE - POINT

PERSPECTIVE THEORY

A number of fundamental considerations must be made before any perspective can be drawn. These considerations affect the final perspective drawing's emphasis, size, and degree of foreshortening. Thus each of these decisions are illustrated because they are pertinent to any type of perspective drawing regardless of the method or construction. The term "point of view" is often used to describe these variables because it suggests that decisions regarding the height of the horizon in relation to the ground plane, the location of the picture plane, and the distance the observer is from the picture plane have been considered. The first variable, the height of the observer in relation to the ground plane determines the location of the horizon and in turn determines if the view will be from above (aerial), normal, or from below.

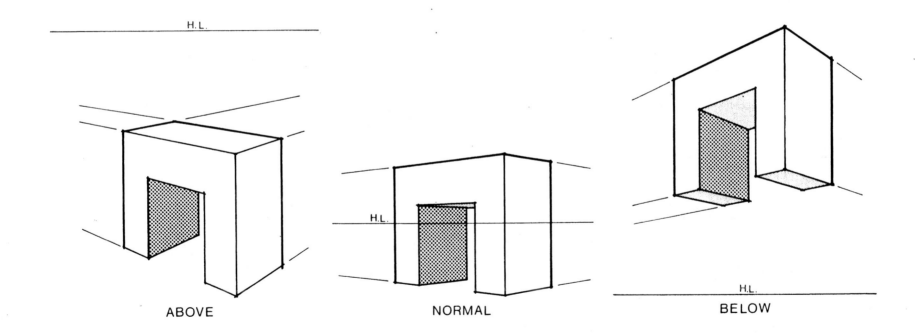

ABOVE   NORMAL   BELOW

PERSPECTIVE THEORY

The location of the picture plane is a critical variable in perspective drawing. If the sight point and object remain fixed, moving the picture plane will alter the size of the resultant drawing. Moving the picture plane closer to the sight point will reduce the drawing size, while placing the picture plane further away from the sight point will make the image larger.

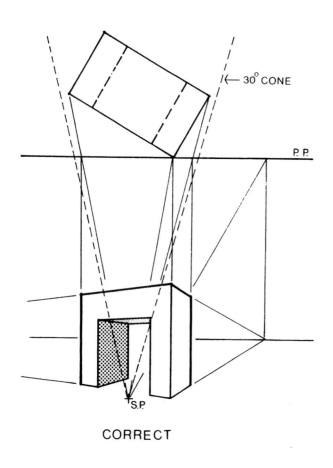

CORRECT

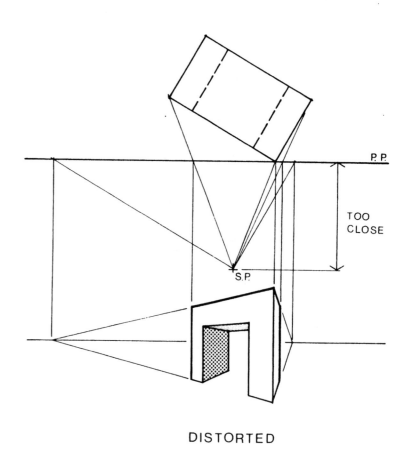

DISTORTED

The distance the observer is from the picture plane determines the proportions of the final perspective image. These proportions are reflected in the amount of foreshortening that appears with lines drawn to vanishing points. If the observer is too close to the picture plane, the vanishing points become close and distortion is apparent, with the resultant perspective image compressed. In order to avoid distortion of this type, most sight points are located using a fixed cone of vision angle. As the sight point moves further away from the picture plane, the vanishing points move further apart and the degree of foreshortening is considerably less.

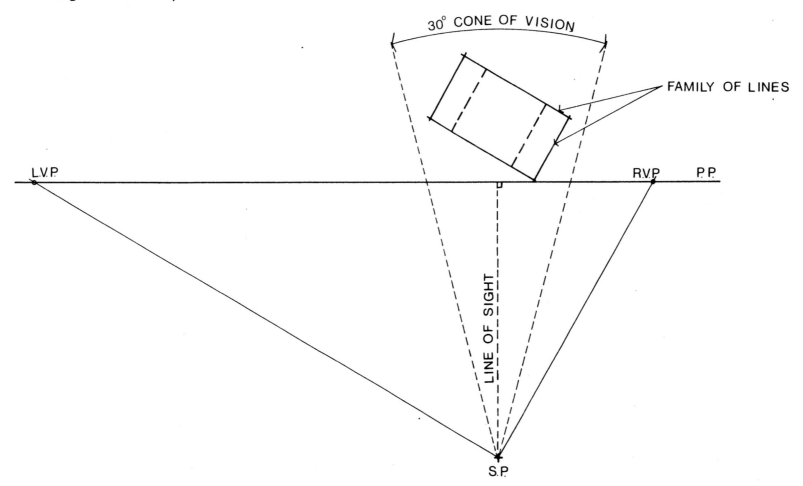

ANGULAR PERSPECTIVE (IN PLAN VIEW)

TWO-POINT OR ANGULAR PERSPECTIVE

There are numerous ways of drawing a perspective. One method relies upon the trained eye to judge convergence, depth, proportions, and is usually performed freehand. Other methods involve the use of analytical systems of various types and construction. These latter methods are referred to as mechanical or analytical perspectives and the two most often used in architecture are: Common or Office Method and Perspective Plan Method. Whatever the method selected, certain basic perspective principles must be understood in order to successfully complete the drawing. For this reason, each method will be described in theory and detail which will allow comparisons to be made on their use and appropriateness. As one becomes proficient at perspective drawing, decisions regarding the choice of methods and any considerations which allow for the speeding up of the process will come naturally. Two-point or angular perspective using the common or office method is described first because it contains many general principles characteristic of all types of perspective. Using this method requires that the plan and elevation be drawn at a convenient scale before the perspective drawing is started. This will influence the size of the final image and should be given more than casual consideration. Once the perspective is completed, it is possible to enlarge the final image, but it is more convenient to make all the orthographic drawings the proper size initially. Before beginning construction of the perspective, consideration should be given to the previous discussion on the effects of sight point, picture plane, and horizon placement.

Beginning in the plan view, the object is positioned with respect to the picture plane. The sight point is located along a line perpendicular to the picture plane at a distance which will allow for the use of a 30° cone of vision. The cone of vision should encompass the entire plan to keep distortion to a minimum. If the object is rectangular, there will be two vanishing points which are located by drawing lines parallel to each family of lines in the plan view from the sight point. Where these lines pierce the picture plane determines the vanishing points.

The layout on this page shows in the plan view only the relationships that exist between the object, picture plane, sight point, and vanishing points. It is in this view that the architect makes many of the decisions that will determine the outcome of the final perspective image.

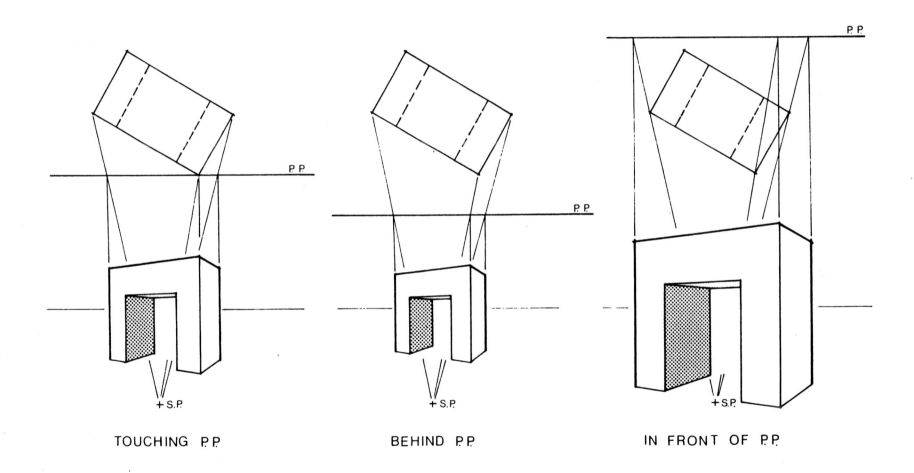

TOUCHING P.P.   BEHIND P.P.   IN FRONT OF P.P.

Before the perspective image is drawn, one final decision needs to be made. The distance the observer's eye is above the ground will determine whether the resultant image is from above showing the top of the object, or from below, or at about five feet as it would normally appear for an observer standing on the ground plane. Selecting one of these positions will determine the placement of the horizon line.

At this point, the preliminary mechanics have been completed and the actual perspective image can be started. Two principles regarding measuring of true height must be followed. (1) If any part of the object touches the picture plane its true height can be measured directly on the perspective image. (2) Any point behind or in front of the picture plane will be smaller or larger in the perspective drawing and therefore cannot be measured in the same manner as principle number one. It must be understood that true height can only be measured when the object is touching the picture plane. If the point in question is either behind or in front of the picture plane, it must be projected to the picture plane so that its true height can be measured and then projected back to its original location. This can be done rather easily if one uses the family of lines and appropriate vanishing points.

The procedure is to identify in plan where the object touches the picture plane. If this does not happen, then principle number two must be used. Through the point project a construction line that is parallel to one of the family of lines used to establish a vanishing point. This line is extended until it pierces the picture plane where its true height is measured and then projected back to its original location. Visual rays drawn from the sight point will establish its location in the perspective drawing. This procedure can be repeated for all points which do not touch the picture plane, but is often modified as one becomes proficient at perspective theory. To complete the perspective, draw visual rays from the sight point to critical points in the plan, and where they pierce the picture plane project orthographically to the perspective drawing.

ANGULAR PERSPECTIVE — OFFICE METHOD

The drawing below illustrates a completed angular perspective using the common or office method.

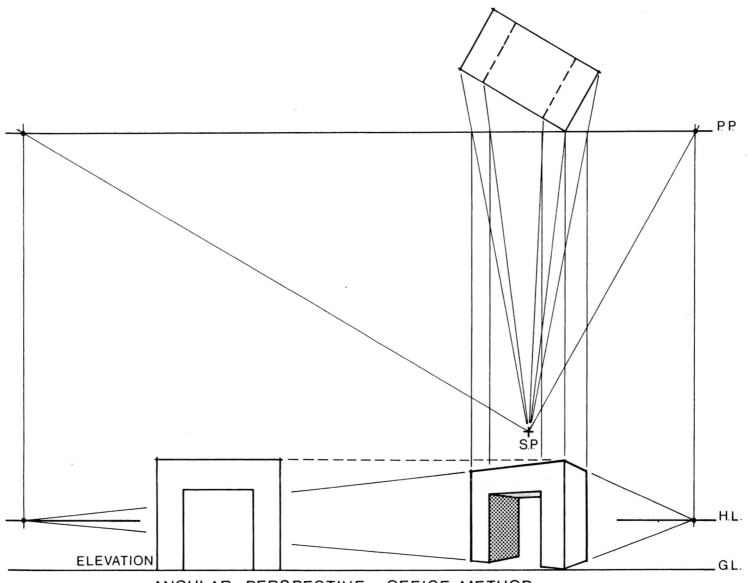

ANGULAR PERSPECTIVE - OFFICE METHOD

Angular Perspective — Office Method

The preceding description and layout of a perspective drawing using the office method described in detail the theoretical procedure for constructing a two point perspective. The theory of perspective and its layout may be more easily understood if the procedure is reduced to a number of fundamental steps. The next several pages illustrate a step by step layout of an angular perspective using the office method. Once these steps are mastered, drawing a perspective of any object from a variety of viewpoints should become automatic. The steps are as follows:

1. Position the plan with respect to the picture plane. The angles selected are usually any convenient angles such as 30, 45 or 60 degrees.

2. Locate the Line of Sight approximately midway through the plan of the object. Along the Line of Sight locate the Sight Point using a 30 degree cone of vision angle. Note: no part of the plan should fall outside of the cone of vision angle or else there could be possible distortion in the final perspective view.

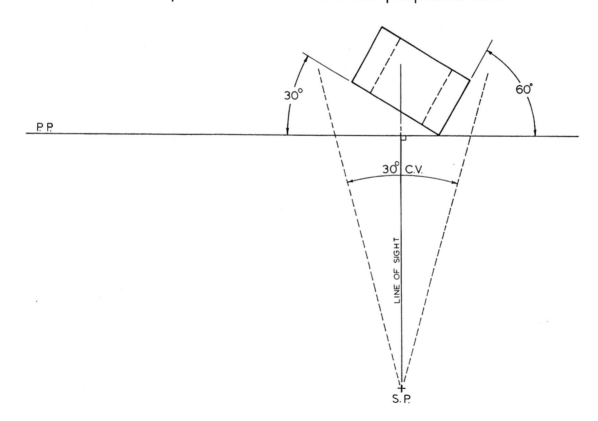

ANGULAR PERSPECTIVE — OFFICE METHOD

3. The previous steps located the Sight Point and other important features of the proposed perspective drawing. Another important item to determine in plan is the location of the two vanishing points. In the object being used there are two families of lines that make angles with respect to the picture plane. Each family will have its own specific vanishing point which can be located in this view. To find each vanishing point, simply draw lines from the sight point parallel to the two family of lines up to the left and right until they pierce the picture plane. The vanishing points are found where these piercing points are located along the picture plane. There will be a right and a left vanishing point for each family of lines.

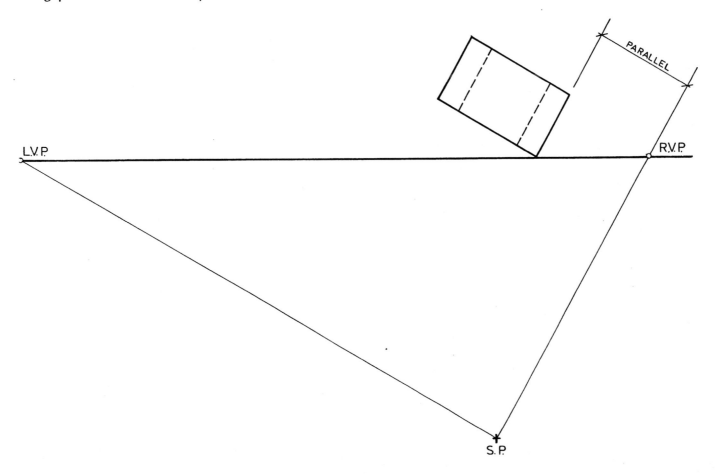

ANGULAR PERSPECTIVE — OFFICE METHOD

4. After locating the relevant information in the plan view it is necessary to move to the elevation view and establish the following: Locate the Ground Line below the sight point. Along the ground line draw an elevation of the object. Next locate the Horizon Line in relation to the ground line. After locating the horizon line project the Vanishing Points from where they are located along the picture plane in plan down to the horizon line. This then completes the necessary placement of all items needed to begin drawing the perspective.

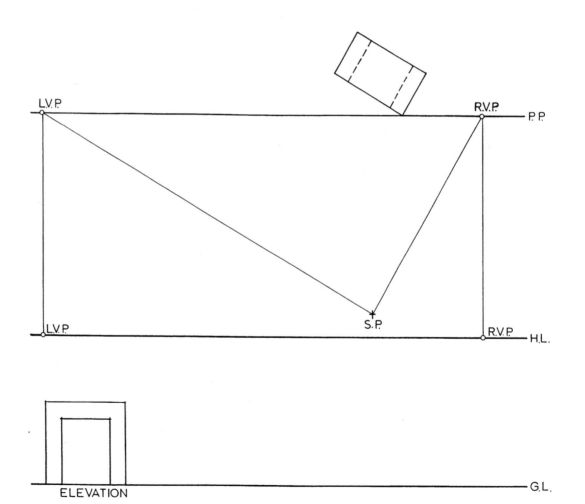

ELEVATION

ANGULAR PERSPECTIVE — OFFICE METHOD

5. In order to draw the perspective it is necessary to recognize that any point in plan that touches the picture plane will appear in true length in the perspective view. In this example, the true height line is the corner of the object and this line is projected into the perspective picture. Once projected the right side of the object is drawn using the true height line to establish the correct height and lines from the sight point to the right corner in plan to work out the exact depth of the object in perspective. Note that in the final step, lines are drawn from the sight point in plan to the right corner and where they cross the picture plane are then projected down to the perspective drawing. This technique will be repeated many times using the office method for drawing a perspective.

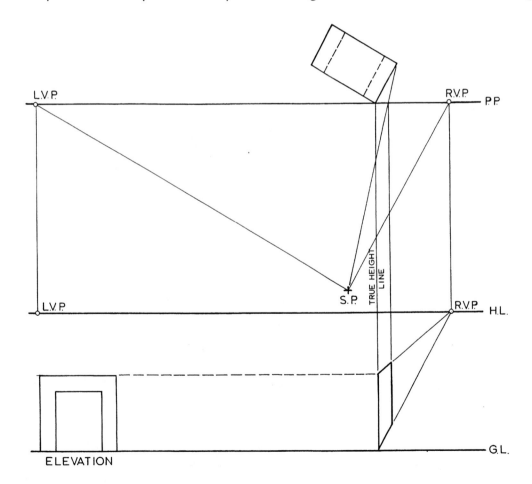

ANGULAR PERSPECTIVE — OFFICE METHOD

6. The left side is then constructed starting from the true height line in perspective and drawing receding lines to the left vanishing point. The depth of the object is determined by drawing lines from the sight point in plan to the left corner and where these lines pierce the picture plane they are projected down to the perspective picture.

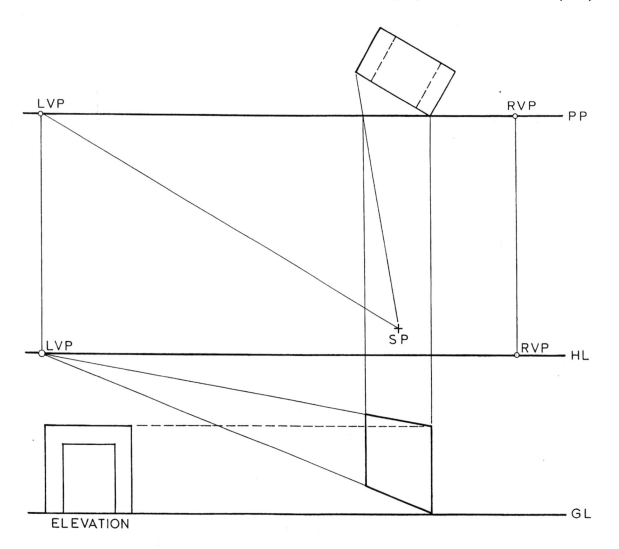

ELEVATION

Angular Perspective — Office Method

7. The top is added by drawing lines from the right and left sides of the object in perspective to the opposite vanishing points. This then completes the overall general view of the object. All that remains to be completed is to add the void which is located in the center of the object.

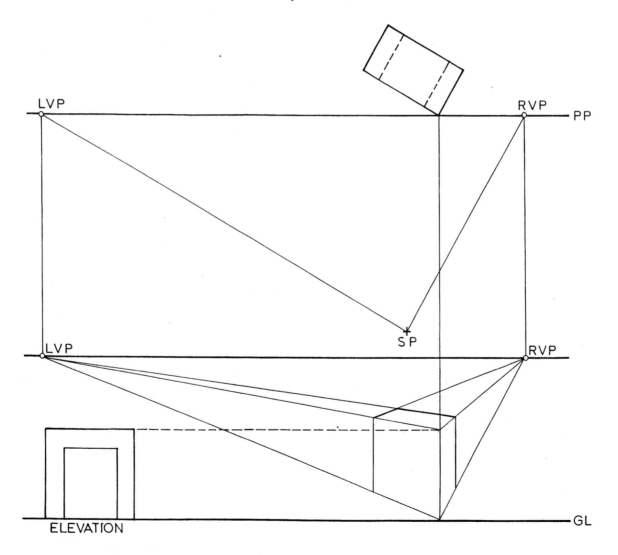

ANGULAR PERSPECTIVE — OFFICE METHOD

8. The final step in the perspective drawing is to add the void in the center of the object. Its true height is projected horizontally across from the elevation view to the true height line. Once located along this line the height of the void is projected to the left vanishing point. Its width is found by drawing lines from the sight point in plan to its exact location in plan. Where these lines cross the picture plane determines the width of the void in plan. This information is then projected down to the perspective image. This then completes the steps necessary to draw this object in perspective.

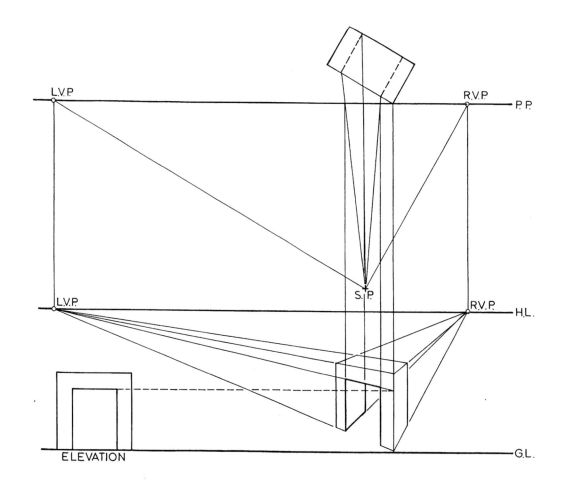

ANGULAR PERSPECTIVE—OFFICE METHOD

In the example given below note how the true heights of the house and tower are established. Although the actual perspective is not complex, numerous vertical lines must be used in order to project from plan view to perspective. Thus in order to maintain accuracy it is necessary that these lines always remain vertical and parallel.

P.P.

+S.P.

H.L.

ELEVATION

G.L.

ANGULAR PERSPECTIVE—OFFICE METHOD

Often the plan of the object will overlap the picture plane in the plan view as shown in the example below. When this happens, the object will project in front of the ground line in the perspective view. The construction of such a situation is illustrated on the given problem where the smaller wing of the building extends past the picture plan.

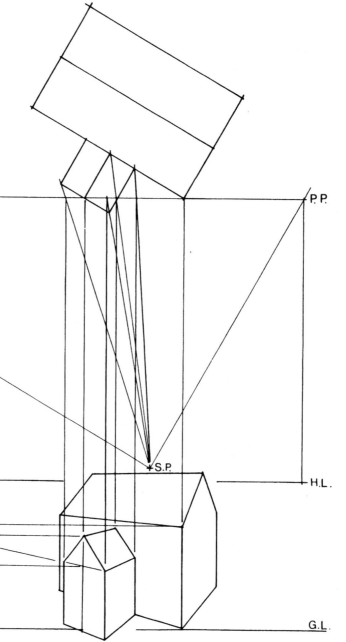

LOCATING POINTS IN PERSPECTIVE

Shown below are two methods for locating the apex of a right pyramid in perspective.

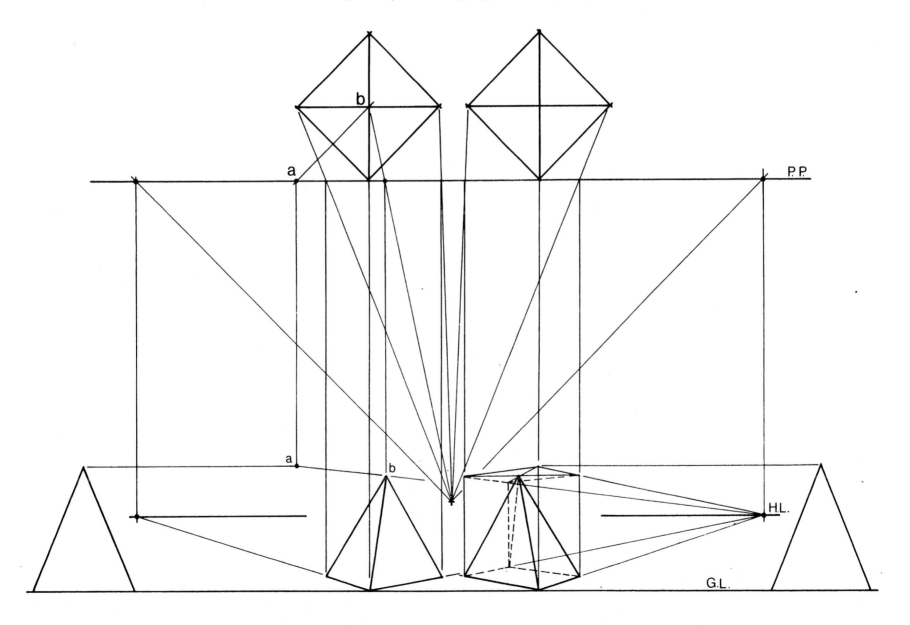

CIRCLES IN PERSPECTIVE

Circles and curves can be drawn in perspective by locating critical points on the curve in both plan and elevation and then finding their appropriate positions in perspective.

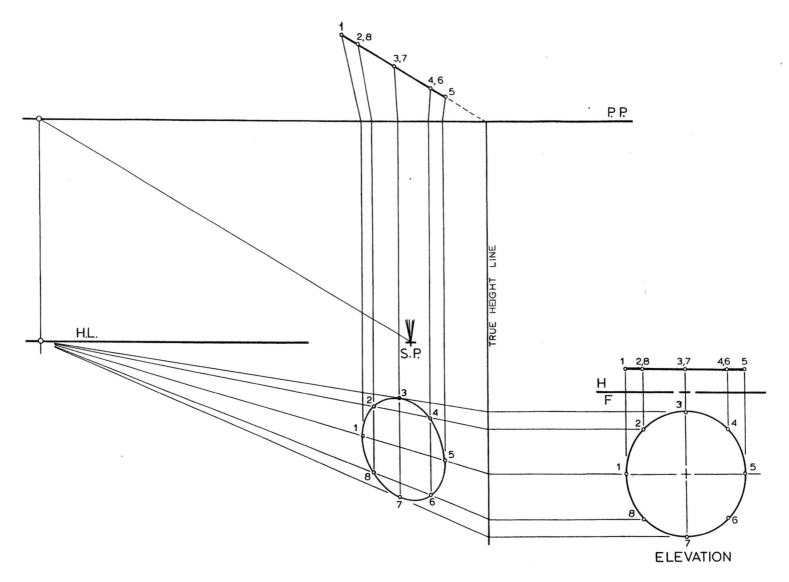

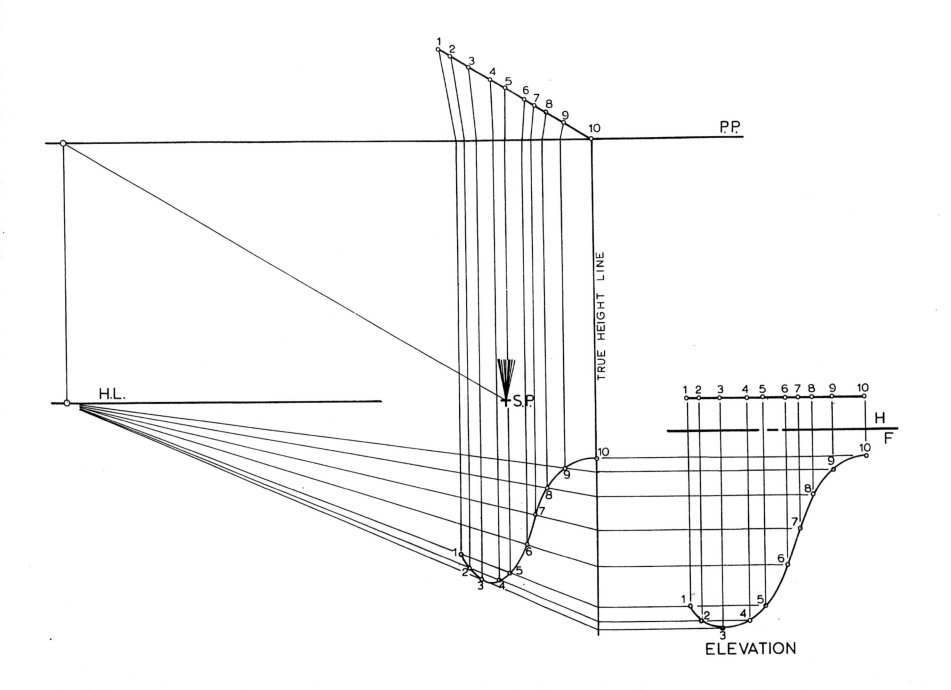

P.P.

TRUE HEIGHT LINE

H.L.

S.P.

H

F

ELEVATION

MULTIPLE VANISHING POINTS

It is possible to have more than the customary two vanishing points in a perspective if the object contains more than two family of lines which make an angle with the picture plane. The drawing below has four vanishing points.

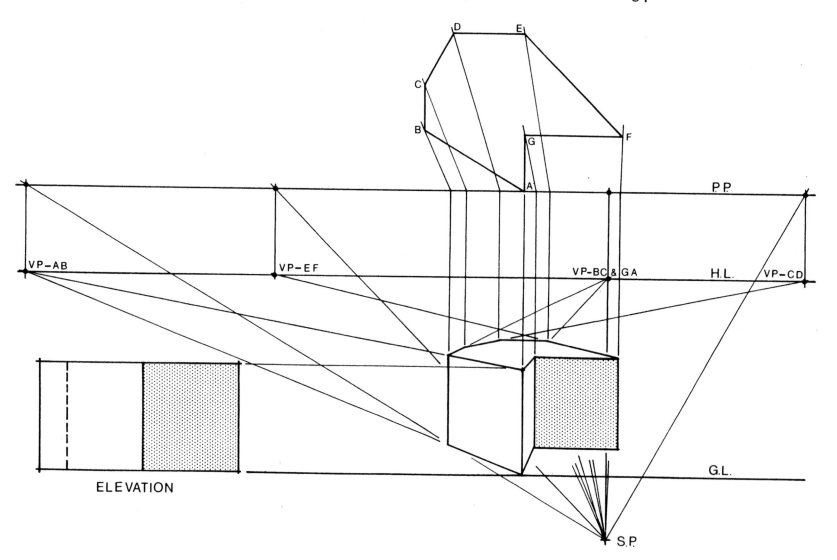

ELEVATION

Vanishing Traces

To locate the vanishing points of lines and planes that are inclined requires that the vanishing trace of these lines or planes be located in perspective. This is done by locating the line of intersection between the picture plane and a plane parallel to the given inclined plane which is passed through the sight point. Since the plan and elevation views are orthographic, rotation is used to measure the true inclination of the trace. A line from the sight point to the appropriate vanishing point is rotated to the picture plane, allowing the true angle of inclination to be measured on the horizon. Once the proper angle is determined, the trace line is extended until it crosses a vertical line drawn from the vanishing point in plan. This intersection will locate the vanishing point for all lines which lie on the inclined plane.

This method of finding the vanishing trace for inclined lines and planes is often used for buildings with sloped walls or roofs, although the vanishing trace most commonly used is the horizon. The visual rays which are parallel to horizontal lines all lie in the horizontal plane through the sight point. Thus the vanishing point of all horizontal lines is on the horizon. This describes the method of locating vanishing points in the plan view for most conventional perspectives. It is only when inclined lines and planes are involved that the vanishing trace is used to locate vanishing points that do not lie on the horizon.

The example on the next page illustrates the method for finding the trace of two inclined planes on a gable roof. The right vanishing point has been omitted from the solution to allow for better visualization.

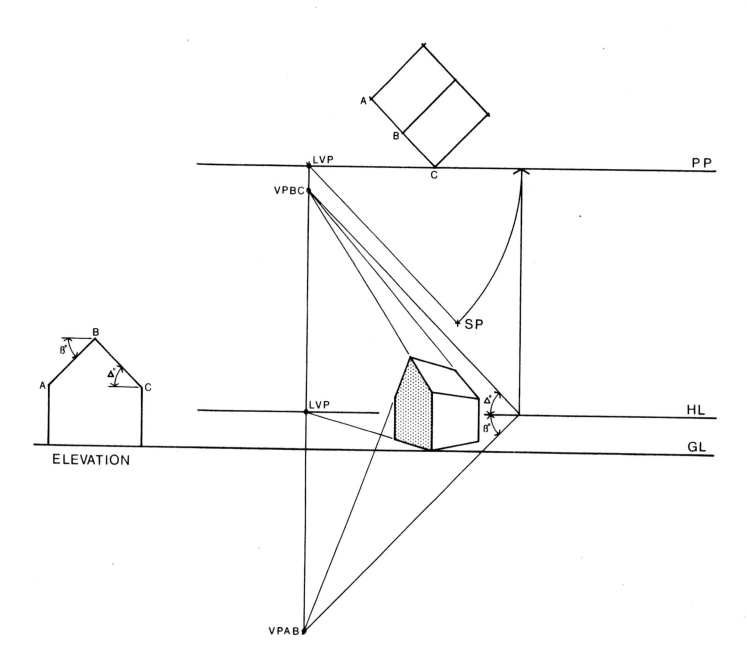

ELEVATION

REPETITION

In perspective it is often necessary to repeat various units. This can be achieved by making use of certain geometrical relationships. The geometry of adding additional cubes to each other is illustrated in the upper example. The lower example uses the same theory to add cubes to each other. Further examples are repeated in Chapter 10 on Perspective Sketching.

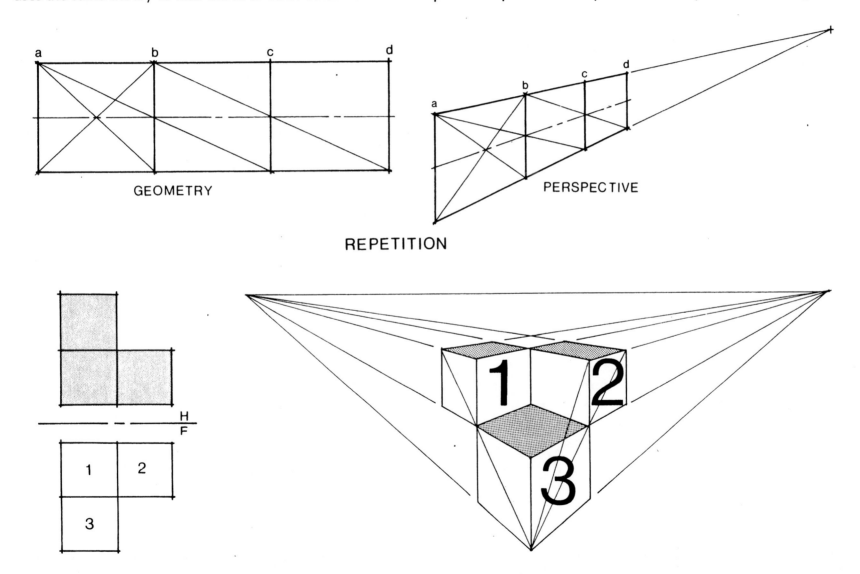

GEOMETRY

PERSPECTIVE

REPETITION

ONE-POINT OR PARALLEL PERSPECTIVE

It is often more effective and convenient to use one-point or parallel perspective instead of two-point. For example, two parallel walls of an interior room and the fronts of buildings on both sides of a street can be shown in one drawing. The only difference between angular and parallel perspective is the position of the object with respect to the picture plane. In parallel perspective, the object is placed parallel to the picture plane thus there is only one "family" of lines that makes an angle with the picture plane and consequently only one vanishing point. In choosing the sight point, distortion can be avoided if the cone of vision angle is approximately 60°. The perspective to the right uses the office or common method for construction.

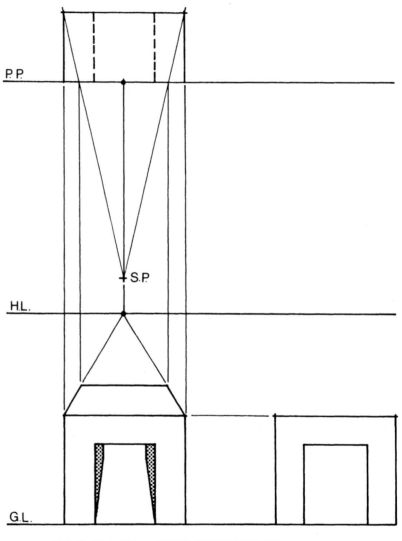

PARALLEL PERSPECTIVE

ONE-POINT PERSPECTIVE OR PARALLEL PERSPECTIVE

The one-point perspective constructed on this page illustrates the technique for drawing a simple perspective. Note the construction for the chimney and how it was located in the perspective drawing.

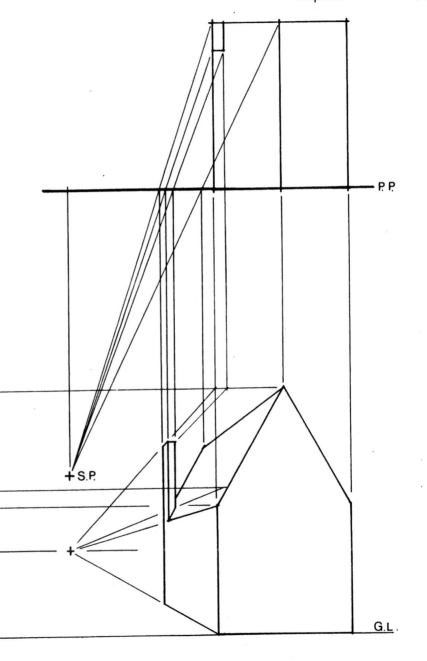

One-Point Perspective or Parallel Perspective

One-point perspective is especially useful for interior perspective because it shows the walls, floors, and ceilings of the room. True heights (h) are measured directly on the picture plane in perspective and projected back to the appropriate location.

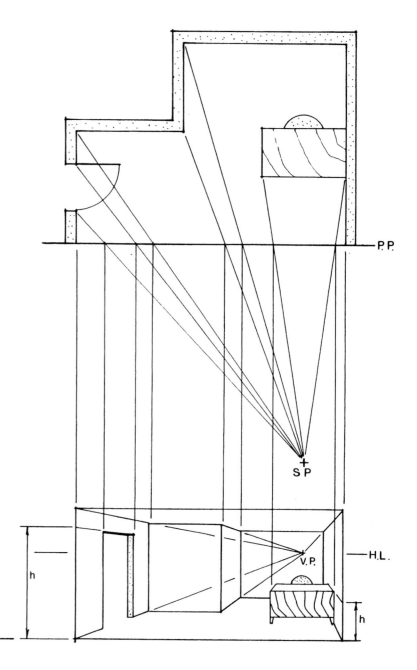

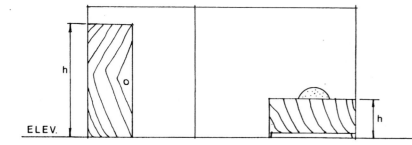

This page illustrates exterior one-point or parallel perspective using the office or common method.

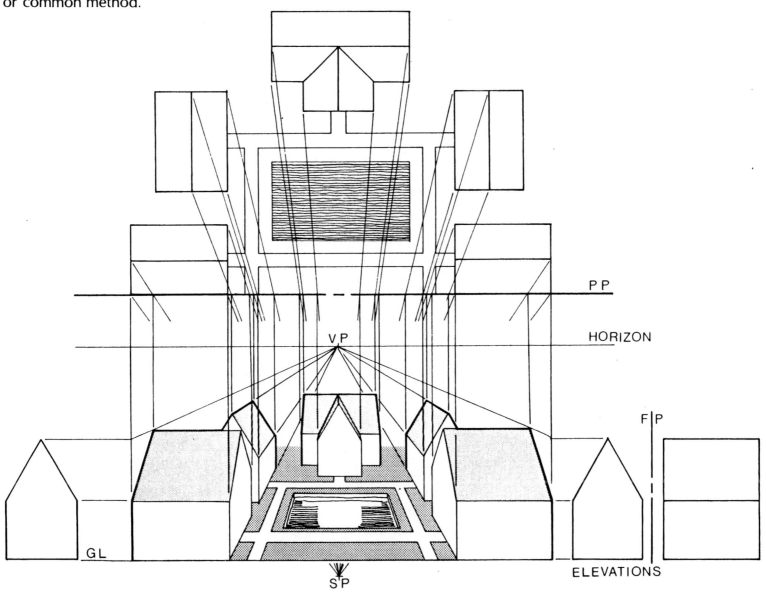

P P

HORIZON

V P

F P

GL

ELEVATIONS

S P

In this one-point perspective example, the picture plane has been placed behind the plan view in order to enlarge the perspective image. Thus the back wall becomes the true height plane and appropriate measurements are then made on the back wall and projected forward. No elevation view is required since all vertical measurements can be scaled directly on the back wall in true height.

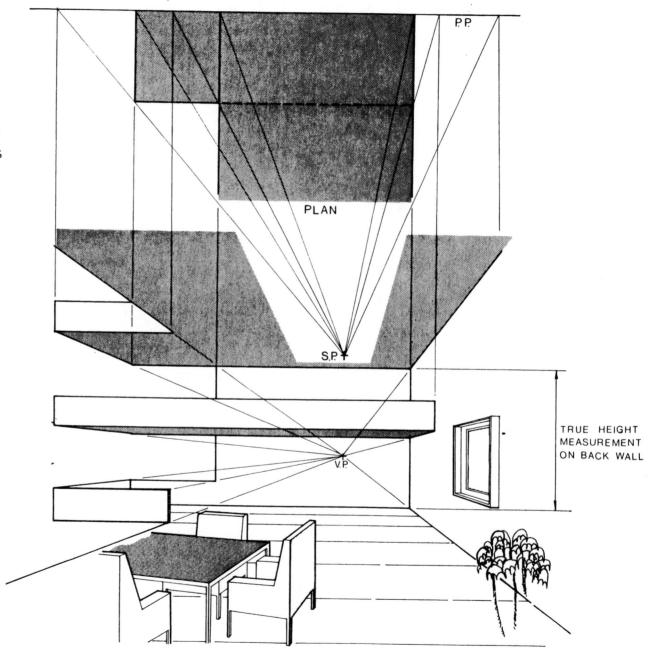

P.P.

PLAN

S.P.

V.P.

TRUE HEIGHT
MEASUREMENT
ON BACK WALL

A unique view from above can be obtained by
reversing the plan and elevation views with the picture
plane. This type of drawing gives the illusion of a three-
point perspective while using one-point techniques, which
are much easier to construct.

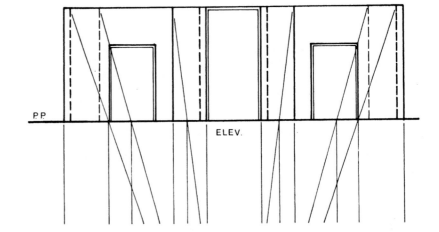

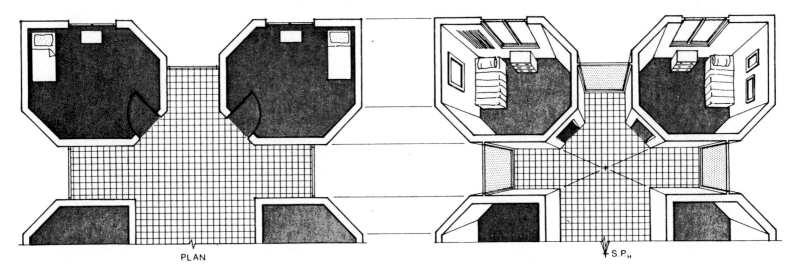

MEASURING POINT METHOD

Another method for drawing a perspective is to use measuring points. Using this method, an actual perspective of the plan of the object is drawn first, and then used for completing the final perspective image. In contrast to the office method, it takes less room on the drawing in the vertical direction. Another advantage is that the plan need not be redrawn in detail when used on the perspective layout. All that is necessary are the proper dimensions of the object. In addition to the customary vanishing points, two additional points are also used. They are called measuring points and are actually vanishing points for the lines that transfer the plan measurements to the measuring line.

The use of the two additional measuring points permits the measuring of a series of direct measurements that can be transferred quickly and accurately to the perspective. The theory for locating measuring points is as follows: A vertical plane is rotated into the picture plane so that direct measurements may be made along the measuring line at the same scale as the plan. In the given illustration on the next page, vertical plane AB is rotated about an axis at A to the picture plane locating point B'. The vanishing point of line B-B' is MPR. Thus MPR is the vanishing point for all lines parallel to B-B'. Because the vertical plane is rotated into the picture plane, measurements in the plan view along the rotated plane will be the same as those used in the perspective drawing. Therefore, the plan view can be eliminated because the width dimensions on the measuring line will equal those in the plan view. A simpler and more accurate method for locating the measuring points is to draw arcs whose radii are equal in length to the distance of the sight point/vanishing point and rotated to the picture plane using the vanishing point as an axis of rotation. (see page 143)

A measuring line is drawn below the ground line along which appropriate distances are measured for corresponding lengths of the plan. Generally the complete plan of the building is drawn in perspective on the measuring line and then used as a method for projecting orthographically to the final perspective drawing. True heights are measured in the normal manner along the ground line.

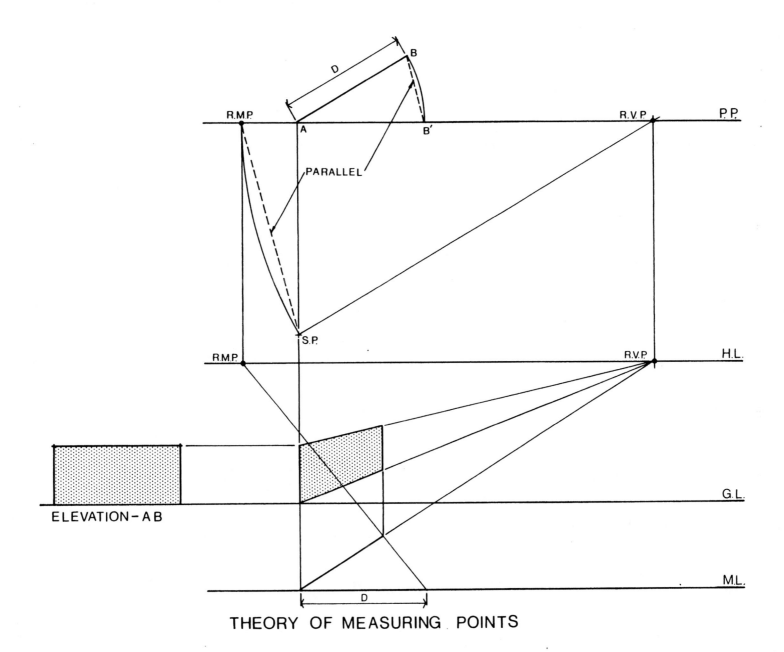

THEORY OF MEASURING POINTS

Illustrated below is a perspective drawing using the measuring point method. Note that the small scale drawing is used only as a means for finding the distances between vanishing and measuring points which are then transferred to the larger perspective drawing.

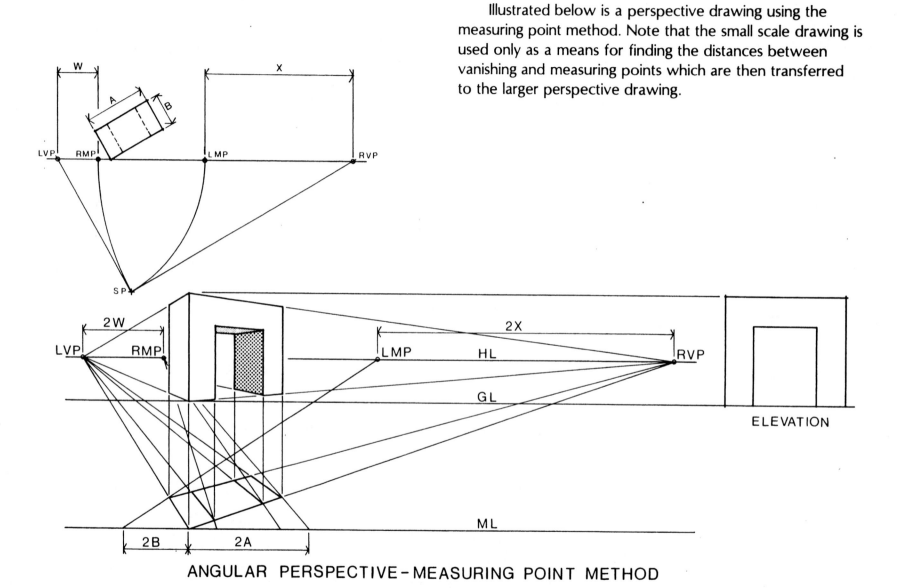

ANGULAR PERSPECTIVE - MEASURING POINT METHOD

This page illustrates how to measure plan distances which lie outside the base lines. Note that point "X" must be located before the wing which lies outside the base lines can be drawn.

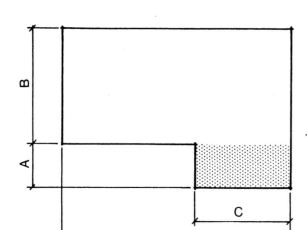

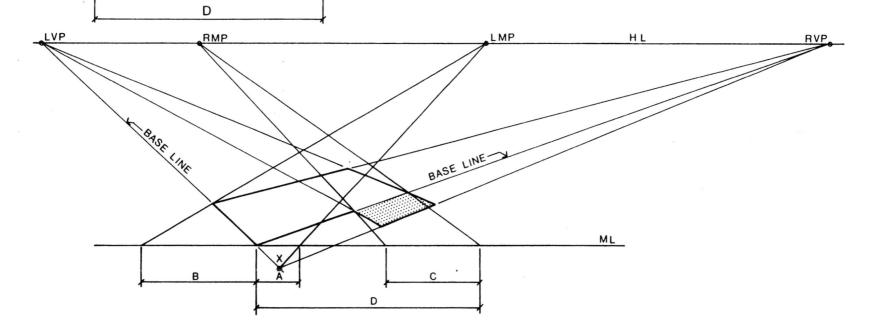

The measuring point method is also applicable for parallel or one-point perspectives. If the measuring line is placed below the ground line, then a perspective of the plan can be drawn and used to complete the perspective image. The sight point is located using a 60° cone of vision and the measuring point is found by rotating the sight point to the picture plane. This point is then located on the horizon at the appropriate scale. Depth distances are transferred to the base line and widths are measured directly on the measuring line and projected to the ground line where they are transferred via the vanishing point to the perspective image. The small scale drawing shown below illustrates how the measuring point and vanishing point are determined. The completed perspective is shown on the next page.

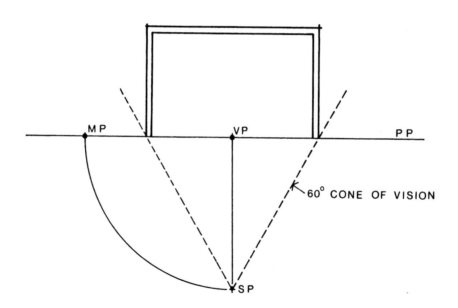

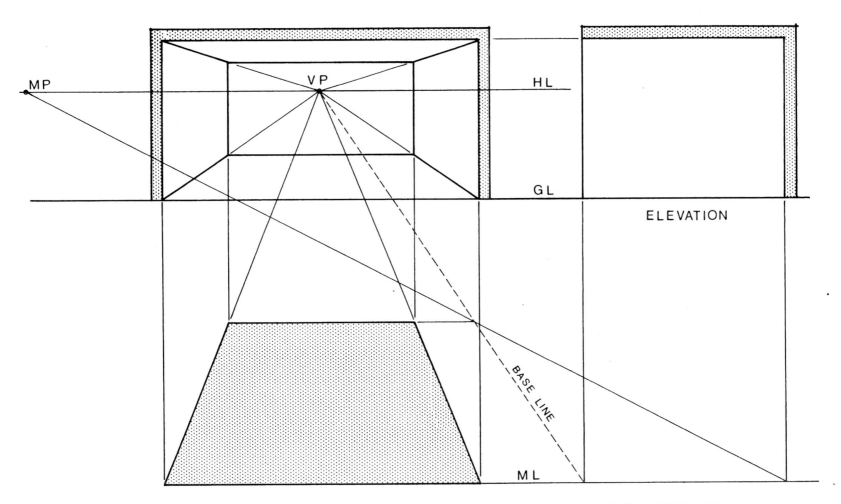

HL

GL

ELEVATION

BASE LINE

ML

PARALLEL PERSPECTIVE - MEASURING POINT METHOD

Illustrated is a sectional parallel perspective using a variation of the measuring point method. Assume the measuring point is given and the space is 30' deep with a door located and dimensioned as shown. The sectional perspective is an excellent method for showing the profile of the building structure and the proposed space.

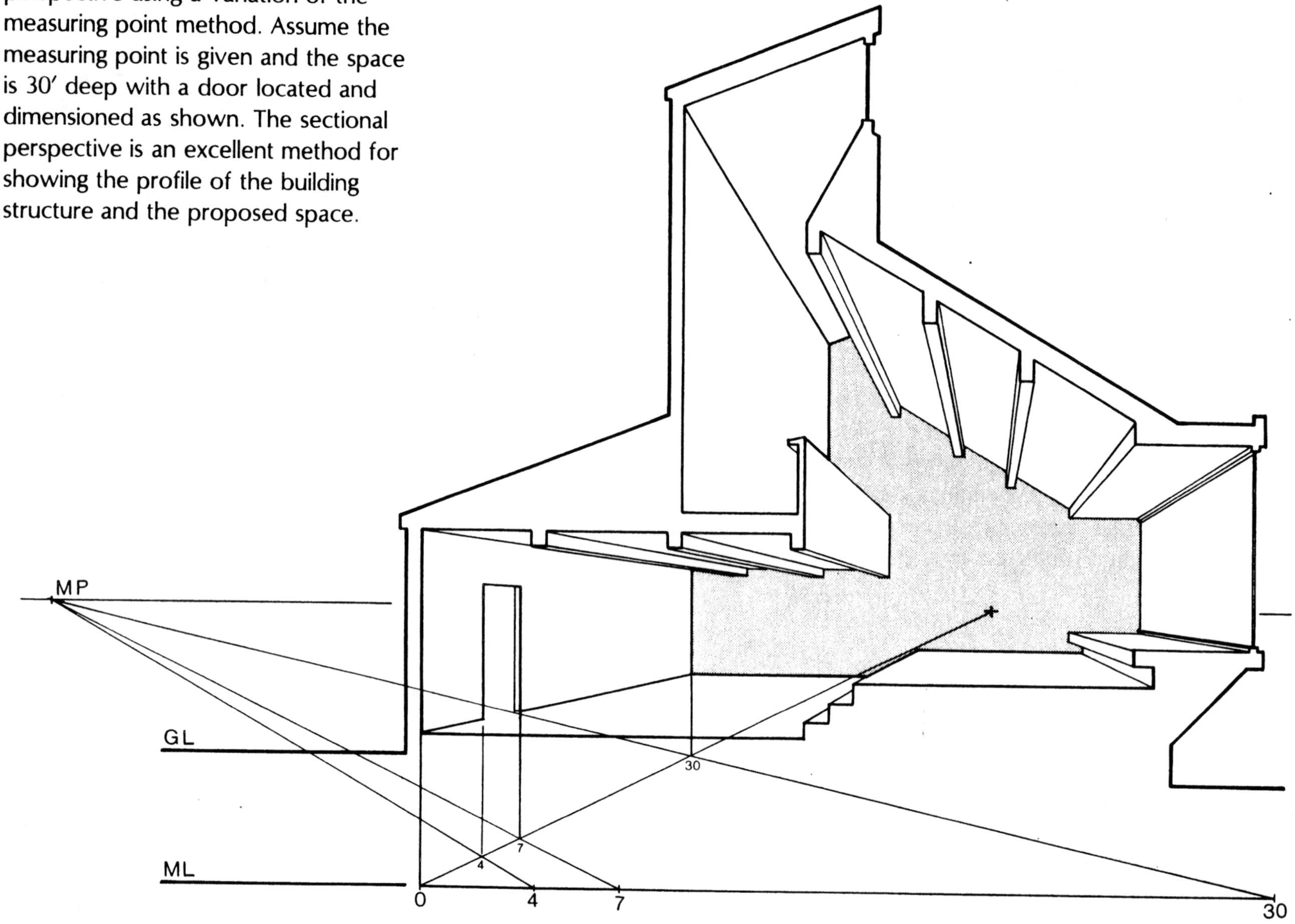

MP

GL

ML

0   4   7   30

THREE POINT PERSPECTIVE

Three point perspective is probably the least used of the various types of perspective drawings because it is more involved in construction and theory. One naturally perceives vertical lines as vertical and therefore two point or angular perspective is perfectly acceptable for most architectural expression.

The theory of three point perspective as illustrated on the next two pages is best described using orthographic projection in a multi-view drawing. (1) First, the plan and profile views must be drawn at the proper scale and positioned in appropriate alignment. The sight point is located in the profile view and the picture plane is drawn perpendicular to the center of vision which is constructed through the center of the object. Because the picture plane must be vertical in a multi-view drawing, it is rotated to a vertical position in the profile view. (2) When the plane is rotated it will move from its original position to a new vertical one so that it will no longer appear to coincide with the ground line in the plan view. This will cause the plan to shift and must be redrawn so that it reflects the rotated profile view. The picture plane will appear to cross the base of the object in the profile view and can now be seen as an edge in the plan view.

Once the plan is redrawn, the sight point is located orthographically in the plan view with its distance equal to that of the profile view. (3) The right and left vanishing points are determined in the plan view by drawing from the sight point parallel to the family of lines until they intersect the picture plane. The third or vertical vanishing point is located by drawing parallel to the remaining family of lines in the profile view and noting where an extension from the sight point pierces the picture plane. This third vanishing point is then projected until it crosses a vertical line drawn from the sight point in the plan view. (4) To complete the perspective image of the object, visual rays are drawn to each critical point from the sight point in both the plan and profile view and projected orthographically to the perspective image.

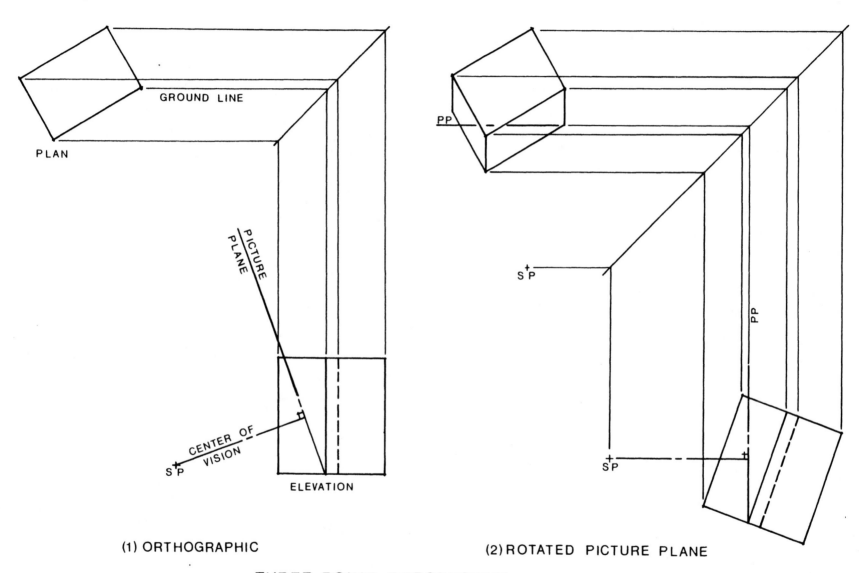

(1) ORTHOGRAPHIC

(2) ROTATED PICTURE PLANE

THREE POINT PERSPECTIVE

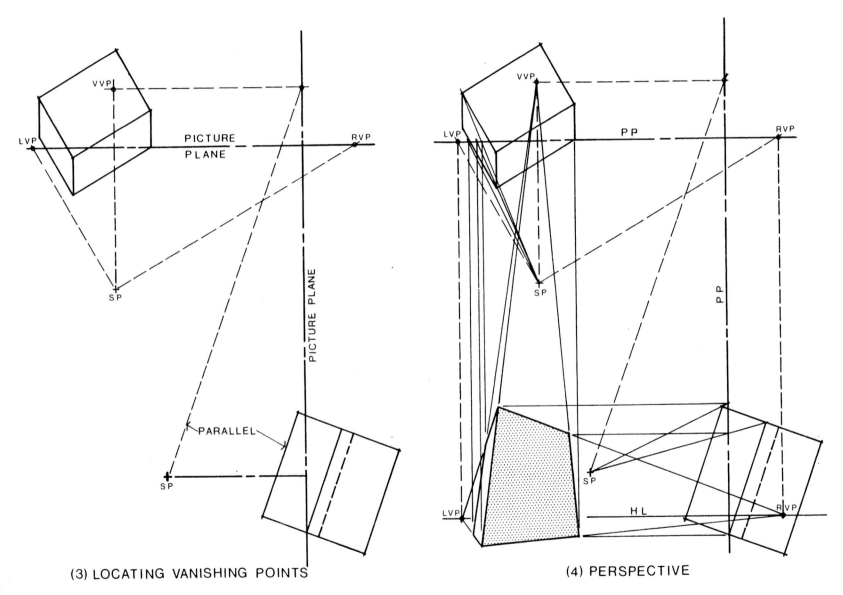

VVP

LVP   PICTURE
                       PLANE   RVP

SP

PICTURE PLANE

PARALLEL

SP

(3) LOCATING VANISHING POINTS

VVP

LVP   P P   RVP

SP

P P

SP

LVP   H L   RVP

(4) PERSPECTIVE

THREE POINT PERSPECTIVE

THREE POINT PERSPECTIVE APPEARANCE

Often one can achieve the effect of a three point perspective using only two vanishing points if the perspective is rotated such that the horizon line is vertical which means that vertical lines will now vanish to a point. It is obvious that the traditional arrangement of plan and perspective image have been rotated 90°.

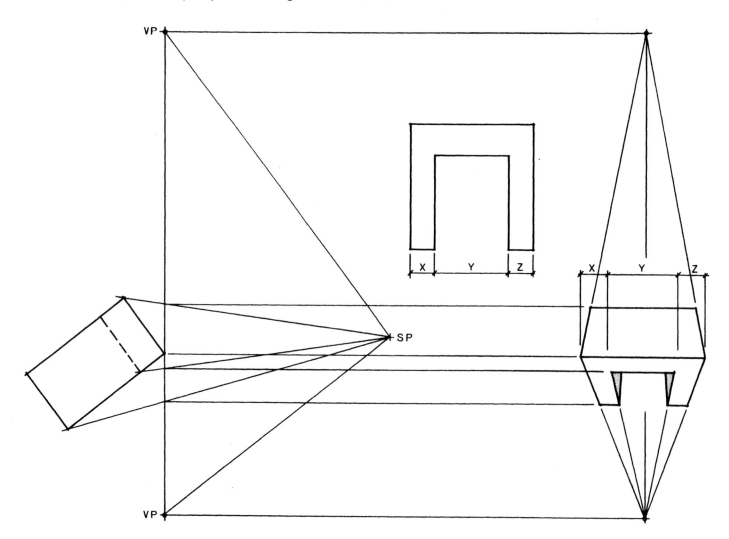

CHAPTER 10

PERSPECTIVE SKETCHING

PERSPECTIVE SKETCHING

In his book, ''Drawing as a Means to Architecture,'' William Kirby Lockard describes a method for perspective sketching which provides a quick freehand method for studying architectural space. It is an excellent process to use as a study aid, but is not intended for use as a precise analytical method. The key to its use is an ability to structure space by subdividing vertical and horizontal surfaces into units of measurement which allow for the use of a grid or coordinate system. Although the method is a combination of geometrical and human judgment, it provides a very reasonable approach for indicating spatial relationships.

The method for using this technique is illustrated in a series of step by step drawings. Before beginning, it is important to note that one vanishing point will appear on the drawing and another considerable distance away, so in effect the drawing is an angular perspective but has much of the characteristics of a parallel perspective due to its orientation. First the horizon is located and a five foot distance is located above and below the horizon through which lines gently vanish to the left. These three lines provide the basic frame for the perspective and will establish the size of the drawing. Next the vanishing point is located on the horizon and the right wall is projected forward. This right wall is very acute and vanishes sharply. From the intersection of the back wall plane and the right side plane a 45° diagonal is drawn on the back wall which will locate a width of 10 units. Further diagonals will locate additional 10 foot units until the desired width is reached. Intermediate distances can be found by subdividing the 10 foot module using diagonals. Thus the back wall is essentially a measuring plane which serves to determine the width of the given space.

Once the width of the back wall is determined, the left side wall is projected forward from the vanishing point. It is on this wall that the depth of the perspective must be judged. Care should be taken in estimating the first 10 foot square as all others are made by using diagonals through the horizon. It is suggested that depth judgments should be made along the plane with the least distortion and in this case it is the left wall. Once the critical depth judgments are made on the left wall, the grid can be completed on the floor or ceiling by sketching lines which are almost parallel to the implied left vanishing point. If the perspective image recedes behind the measuring plane, it is possible to use diagonals to estimate further 10 foot squares. With practice, one can become adept at positioning the variables to obtain an appropriate representation of the space or spaces.

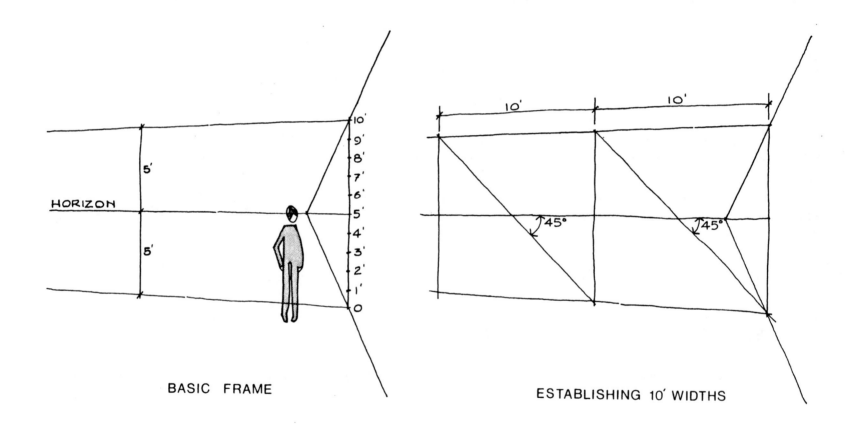

HORIZON

BASIC FRAME

ESTABLISHING 10′ WIDTHS

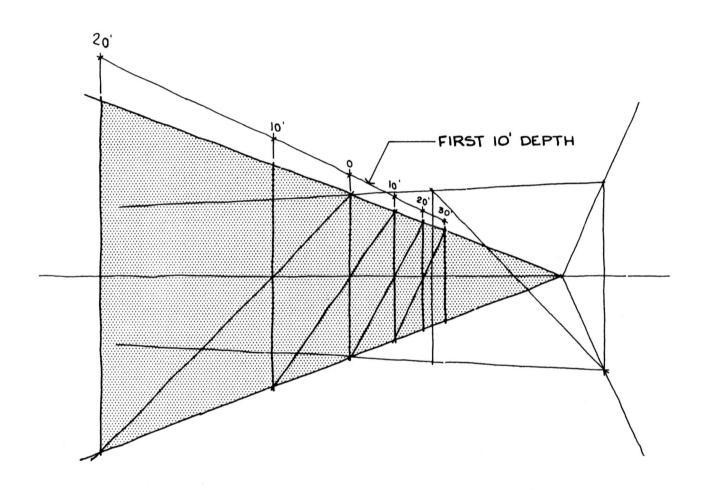

LOCATING 10′ DEPTHS

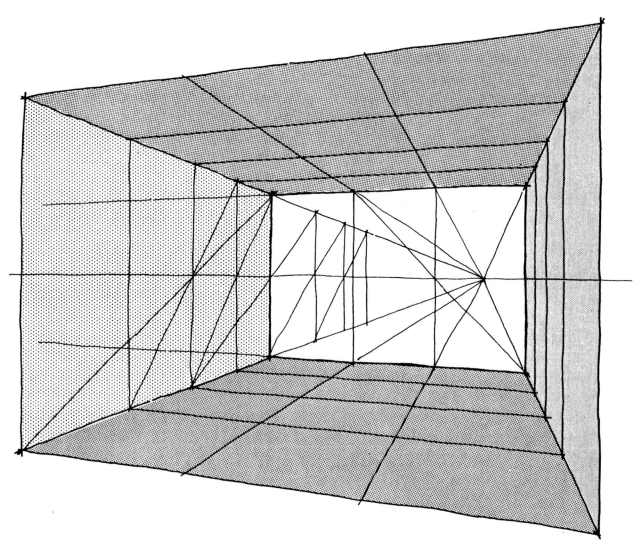

COMPLETED SPACE – 15'W, 20'D, 10'H – DIVIDED INTO 5' UNITS

COMPLETED SKETCH WITH ARCHITECTURAL IMPLICATION

Illustrated on the next two pages is the process for sketching a space which is 15' wide, 15' deep and 10' high.

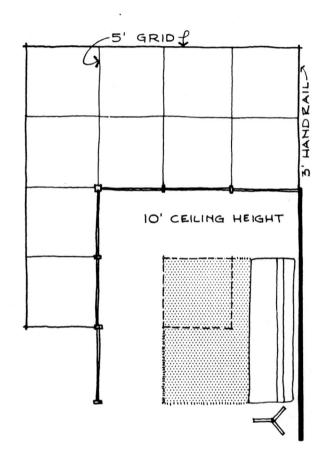

GIVEN SPACE

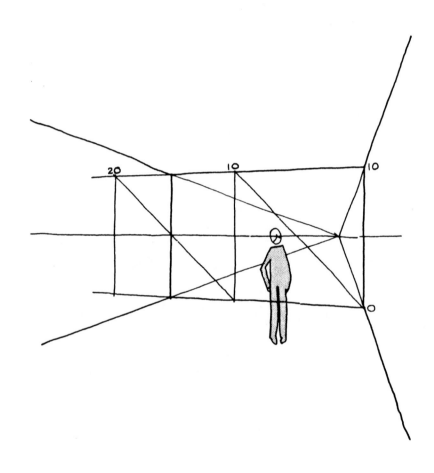

WIDTH JUDGMENT

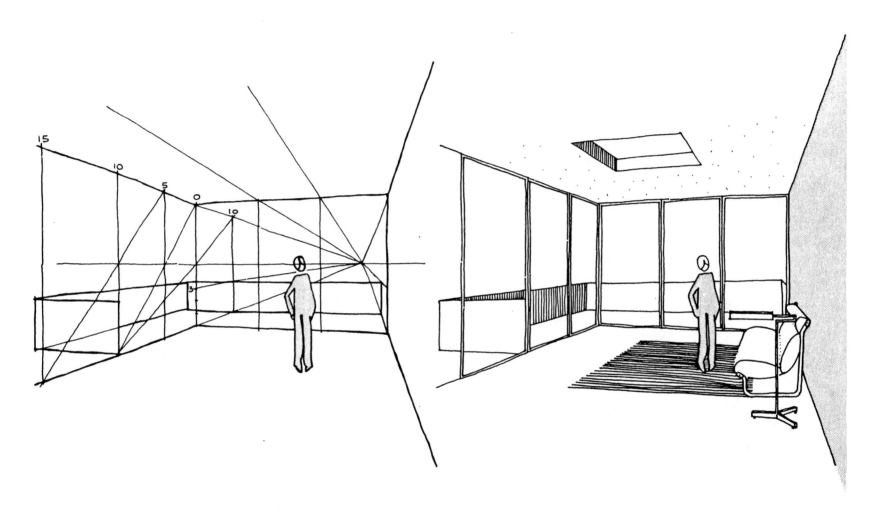

DEPTH JUDGMENT   COMPLETED SKETCH

The examples on this page and the next two pages illustrate freehand sketching in perspective and axonometric. All figures illustrate dividing a cube into a number of critical parts using diagonals as explained in the section on repetition and division in chapter 9.

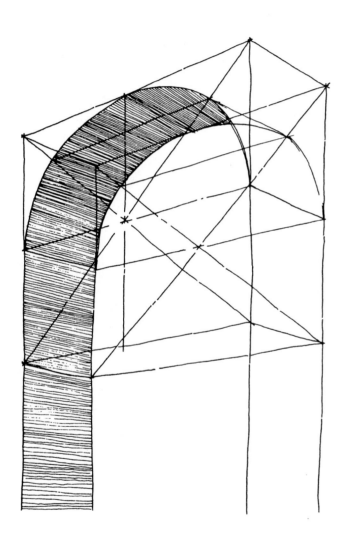

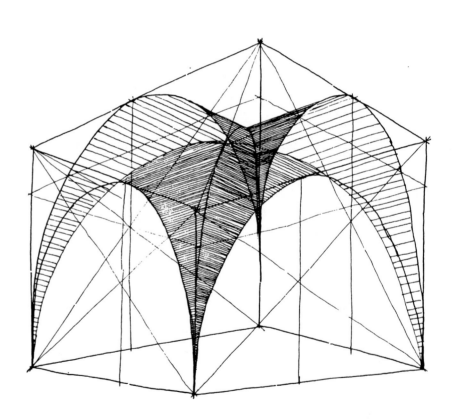

The cylinders shown below illustrate how the cube can be used as a tool for locating critical points on the surfaces of the objects. The geometry of each shape is transfered dimensionally to perspective.

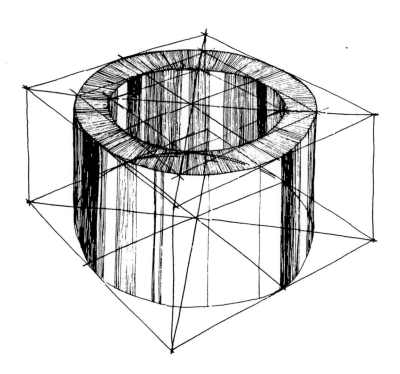
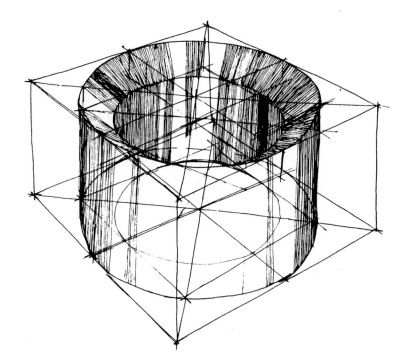

Below are additional examples of freehand sketching in both axonometric and perspective.

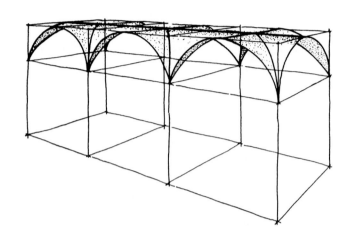

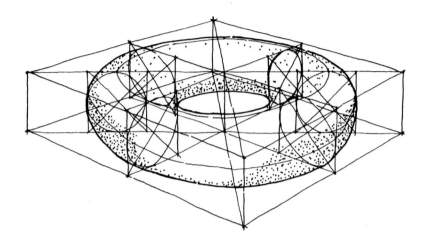

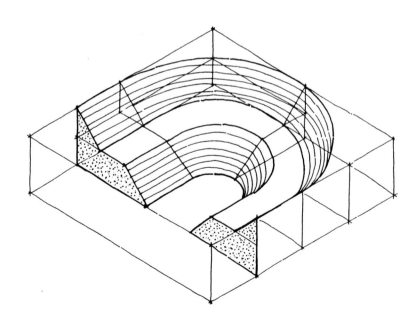

CHAPTER **11**

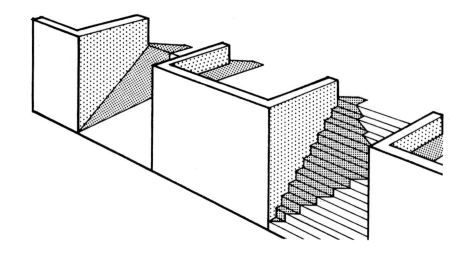

SHADES AND SHADOWS—
ORTHOGRAPHIC AND PERSPECTIVE

It is often possible to add clarity to a drawing by casting shades and shadows. This is achieved by distinguishing details which might otherwise appear flat and anonymous; thus many of the subtleties that might be overlooked can be expressed when shadows are cast. When casting shadows in orthographic drawings it is a common practice to use a standard light ray which has a bearing of N 45° E in plan and sloping 45° in elevation. In this case the sun is assumed to be so distant that all rays will appear parallel. When casting in perspective, the light rays can be parallel or other methods can be used to locate vanishing points so that the rays appear to converge. Whatever methods are used, casting shadows tends to bring another dimension to the drawings.

When casting shadows, the intensity of light is left to the designer's discretion and it is often difficult to determine where shadows end and shade begins. In reality this seems to hold true, thus in order to be consistent the following two principles are used when casting light rays. (1) Shade is caused by the exclusion of light. (2) Shadow is caused by a light ray which has been interrupted by a line or plane which in turn casts a shadow.

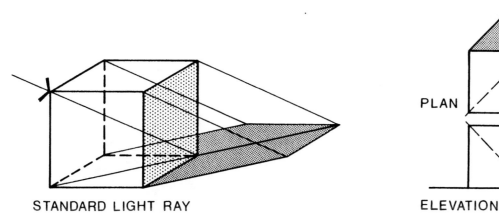

STANDARD LIGHT RAY

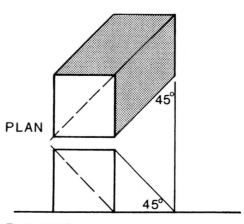

ELEVATION

SHADOWS IN ORTHOGRAPHIC

Normally only the plan and necessary elevation views are needed to cast the shadow line on orthographic drawings. This requires that one completely understands the full meaning of each drawing and is adept at visualizing the object and is capable of making mental transfers from view to view. In order to understand the shadow casting process, the two examples shown below illustrate the procedure in multiview drawing as well as pictorial. Studying both types of drawings provides a method for understanding the procedure for the development of the shadow line. This approach, of using multiview and pictorial drawings together, can be used on a variety of problems when casting the shadow line in plan and elevation.

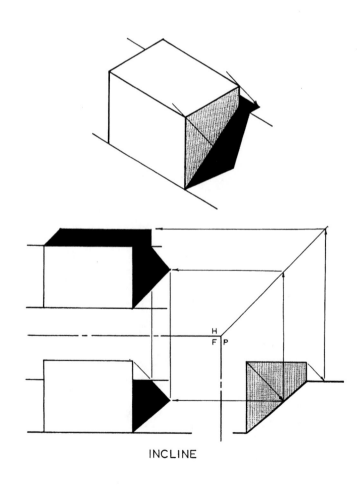

INCLINE

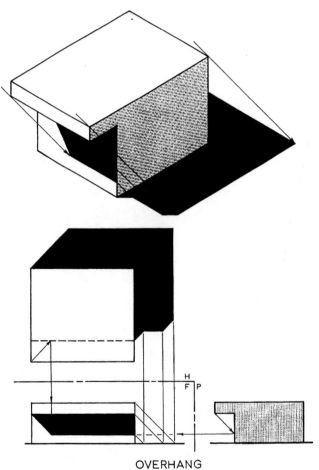

OVERHANG

SHADOWS IN ORTHOGRAPHIC

The following illustrations show several situations where shadows have been cast in orthographic. In all cases, it is apparent that the problem is that of finding the piercing point between the light ray and the planes of the object.

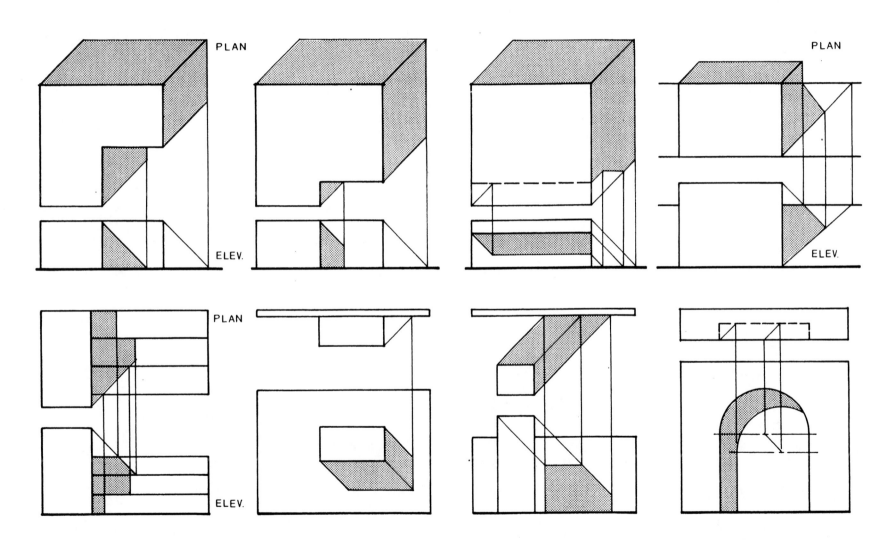

SHADOWS IN ORTHOGRAPHIC

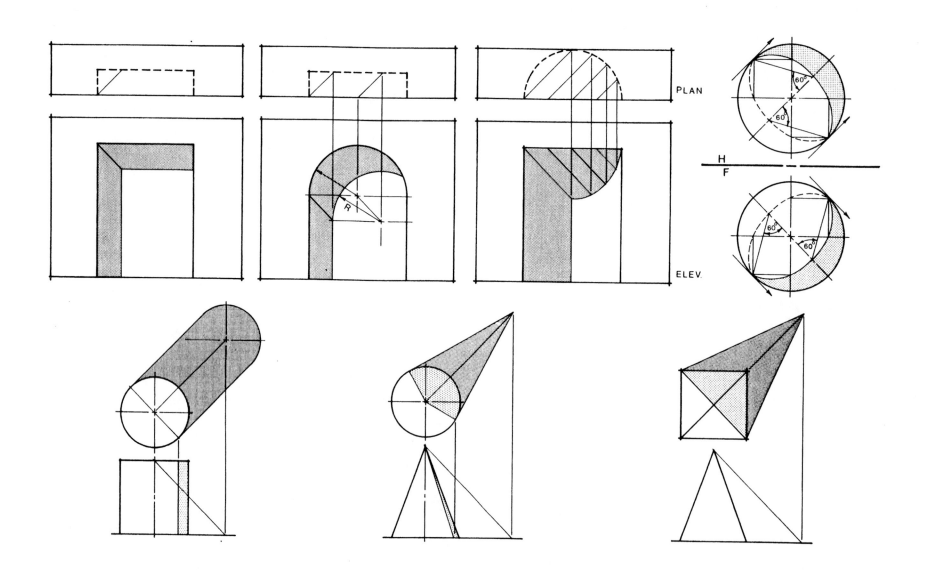

When the three major views of an object are given they can be used to construct the shadow as shown in the two examples below. Only the primary shadows have been determined, and the shade on the side views has not been shown to illustrate construction of the shadow lines.

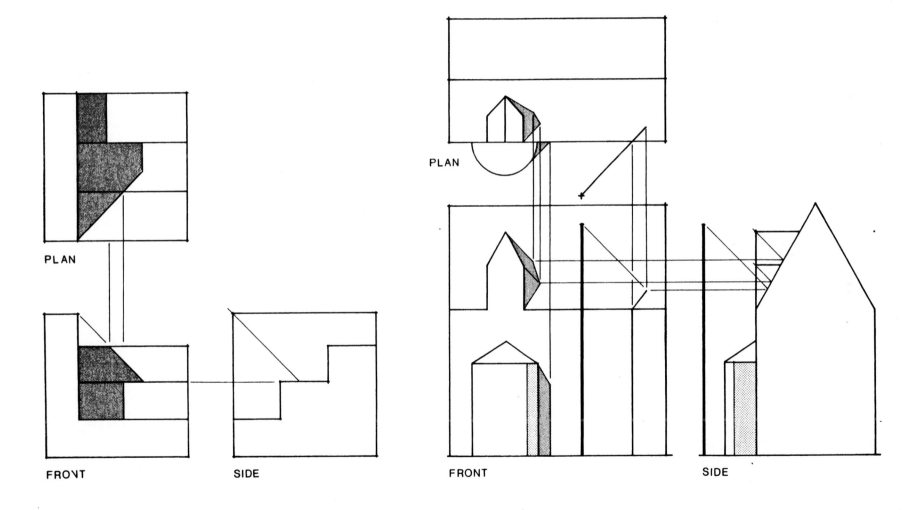

PLAN

FRONT   SIDE

PLAN

FRONT   SIDE

A three view
drawing showing
construction, shade,
and shadow.

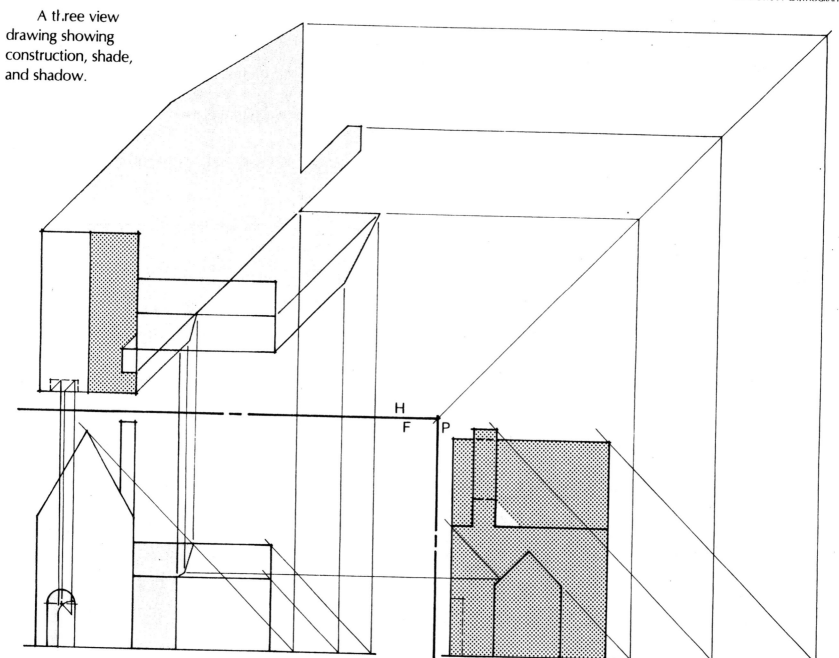

SHADES AND SHADOWS IN PERSPECTIVE

In perspective drawing the lines alone suggest shape and form in three dimensions, but the addition of shades and shadows correctly placed make the drawing more realistic and easier for the observer to judge the true qualities of the design. There are two approaches to casting shades and shadows in perspective; the first is based upon the theory of parallel light rays and the second uses vanishing points for the rays. Regardless of the type selected, there are two fundamental principles of casting shades and shadows in perspective:

1. A vertical line casts its shadow on the ground or on any horizontal surface, in the direction (bearing) of the rays of light. See line AB below.
2. The shadow on a plane, cast by a line parallel to that plane, is parallel to the line. See line BC below.

In the drawing below, vertical lines cast shadows parallel to the picture plane since the light rays are considered parallel. The choice of the angle of light ray is dependent upon the time of day and the season of year, but is usually selected by the designer to best show the effect created by the sun on the design. Horizontal lines will cast shadows that are parallel to the ground and in perspective will vanish to the appropriate vanishing point.

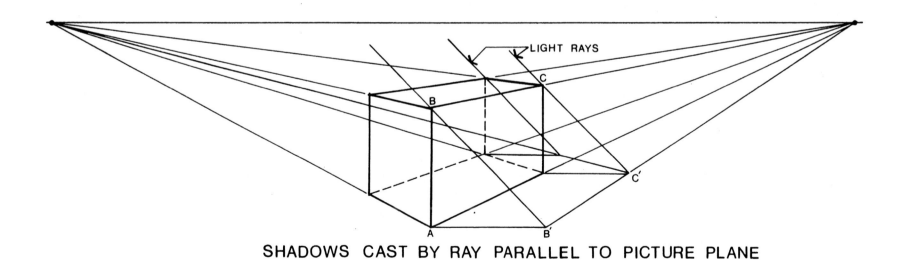

SHADOWS CAST BY RAY PARALLEL TO PICTURE PLANE

The drawings below show the shadows of horizontal and vertical lines falling partially on level ground and partially on a vertical wall.

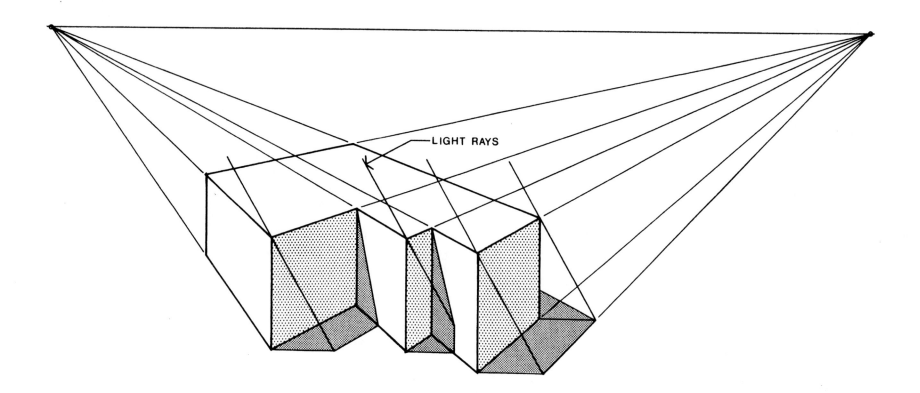

The solution for casting shadows of overhangs is to find the height of the projection above the ground plane and then cast the visible portion of the overhang on the building or ground.

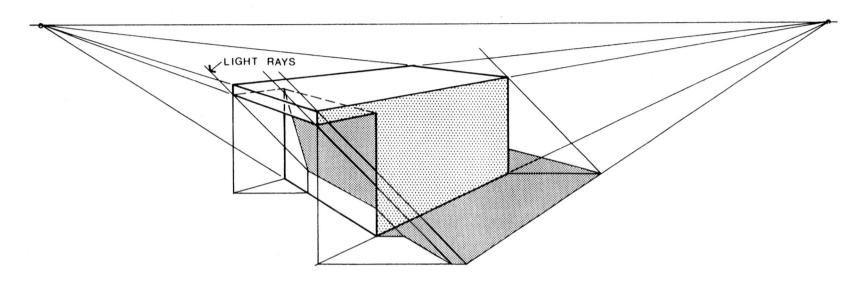

When casting shadows on sloping surfaces it is necessary to find the piercing point of the light ray and the inclined surface. A cutting-plane is passed through the sloping surface at the corner to locate the piercing point.

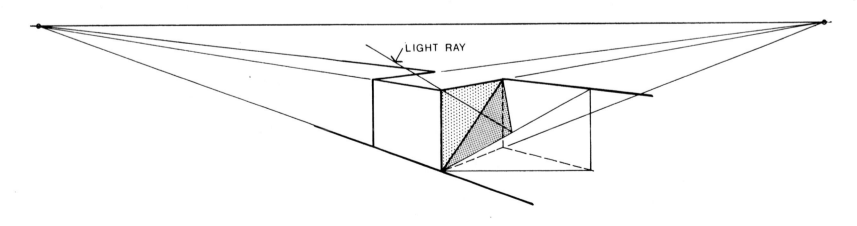

SHADOWS IN PERSPECTIVE

Given the simple hip roof building shown below: in order to obtain the solution, it is first necessary to cast the shadow of point "A" on the ground to see if it falls beyond the shadow of edge B-C. As a first step point "A" must be projected to the ground and then cast along the ground to find how far its shadow line will extend. If the shadow of point "A" extends beyond the shadow line of B'-C', as it does in this example, it will be a part of the final shadow pattern. This also means that roof segment ABC in the perspective drawing is in shade because point "A" is high enough to cast a shadow on the ground.

Had the shadow of point "A" fallen inside or to the left of shadow line B'-C' on the ground, the perspective roof segment ABC would have been in sun. This is because the perspective edge B-C would take precedent over point "A" and would be the only edge which casts on the ground.

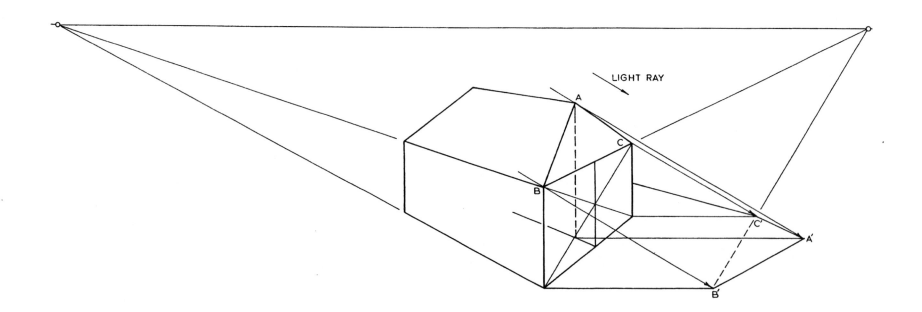

The two examples below illustrate the construction necessary to construct the shadow line when the light ray is parallel to the picture plane.

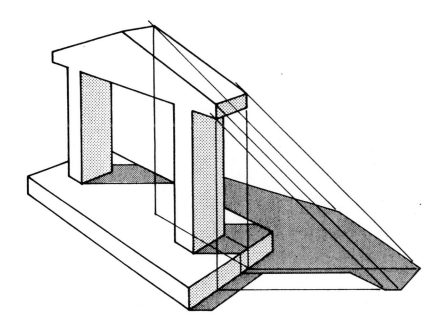
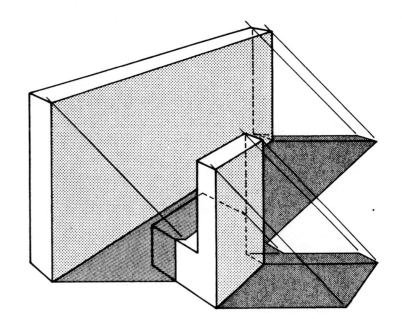

This example illustrates construction of the shadow line plus the use of value to indicate shade and shadow.

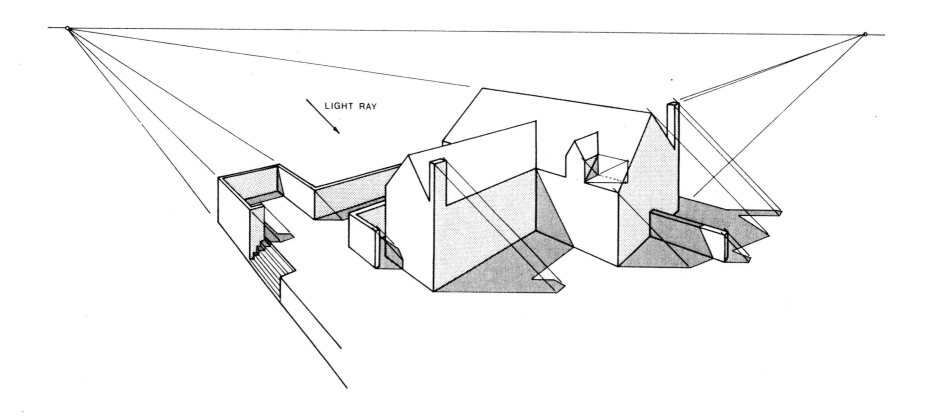

The example below illustrates casting shades and shadows in perspective using a light ray which is parallel to the picture plane.

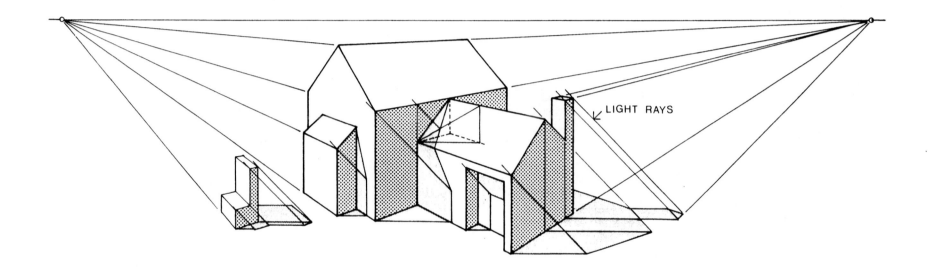

LIGHT RAYS

Illustrated below is an application of casting shades and shadows in perspective on a building with a light ray which is parallel to the picture plane.

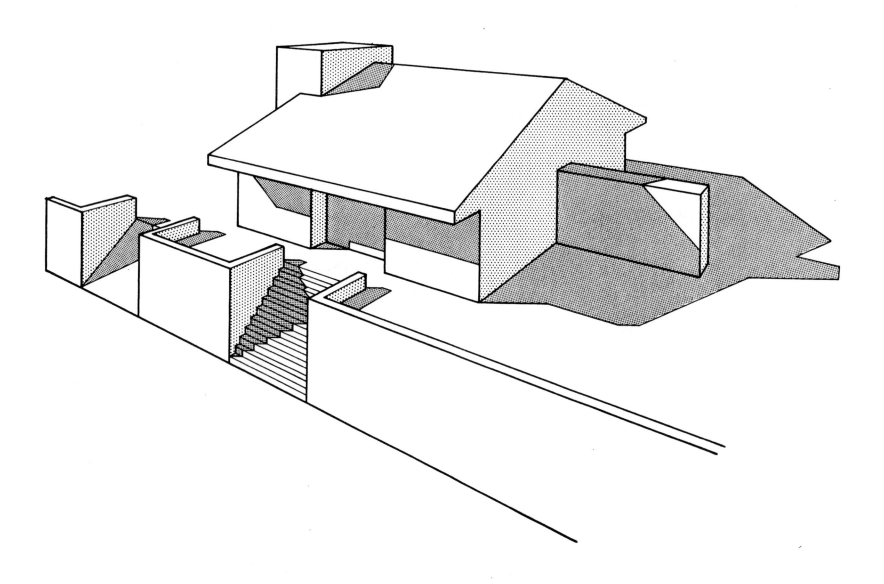

Shades and Shadows with Oblique Light

Up to this point, with the light rays parallel to the picture plane, it has been possible to cast shadows without locating the vanishing points for the sun's rays. This has provided a convenient method, accurate enough for general purpose work, but not technical enough for detailed design drawings. Thus for more accurate information such as the proper size and placement of overhangs and windows on a building, it is suggested that shadows be cast using the actual sun ray angles and azimuth. This means the bearing or azimuth for the light rays need to be determined along with altitude or the angle that the light ray makes with the horizon. This information is available in any universal sun chart which gives data for any hour of any day of the year for any place in the world. Other tables will give similar information for specific latitudes and longitudes in the United States.

In drawing shadows cast by light rays oblique to the picture plane, the principles involved are the same as for light rays that are parallel to the picture plane. The only difference is in establishing two additional points for the direction of the light (or azimuth in plan, LD-VP) and the slope angle (or altitude, LR-VP) for the sun's rays. The procedure for locating the LD-VP is to plot the direction of the light ray in plan from the sight point. This line is extended until it pierces the picture plane. At this intersection, a line is drawn to the horizon which locates the LD-VP. The LD-VP is the point on the horizon where the shadows of all vertical lines converge.

In locating the LR-VP it is necessary to construct the true slope angle of the light rays in a true length elevation view. This can be accomplished by using rotation as a method of construction. In the plan view, the direction of light is rotated into the · picture plane. This will make the elevation view of the line in true length allowing for the exact measurement of the slope angle. The true angle is measured from the horizon and extended until it crosses a line projected vertically from LD-VP. As a check, the final position of the LD-VP and LR-VP should be in vertical projection with each other. Once these two points are located, the casting of shades and shadows is the same procedure as light rays parallel to the picture plane.

The theory just described is for any light ray with a bearing or azimuth of north. If the direction of light has a bearing of south, the LR-VP will be located above the horizon and the resulting shadow will project forward in the perspective.

The example below is for light direction N70°E with a slope of 13°.

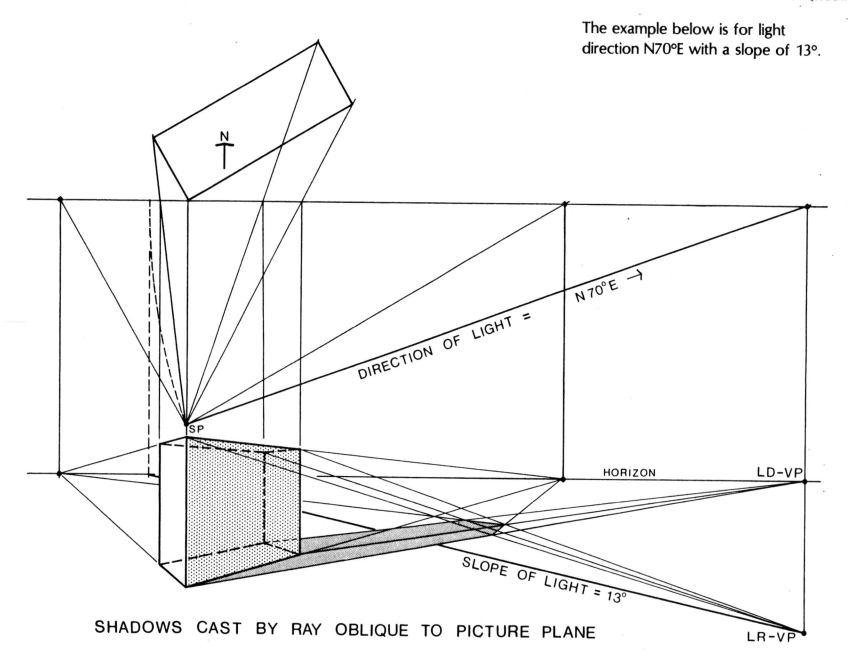

N

DIRECTION OF LIGHT = N 70° E →

SP

HORIZON   LD-VP

SLOPE OF LIGHT = 13°

LR-VP

SHADOWS CAST BY RAY OBLIQUE TO PICTURE PLANE

A light ray with a bearing of South will pierce the picture plane above the horizon before it reaches the sight point. Therefore the LR-VP will be located above the horizon. Illustrated below are two examples of this situation.

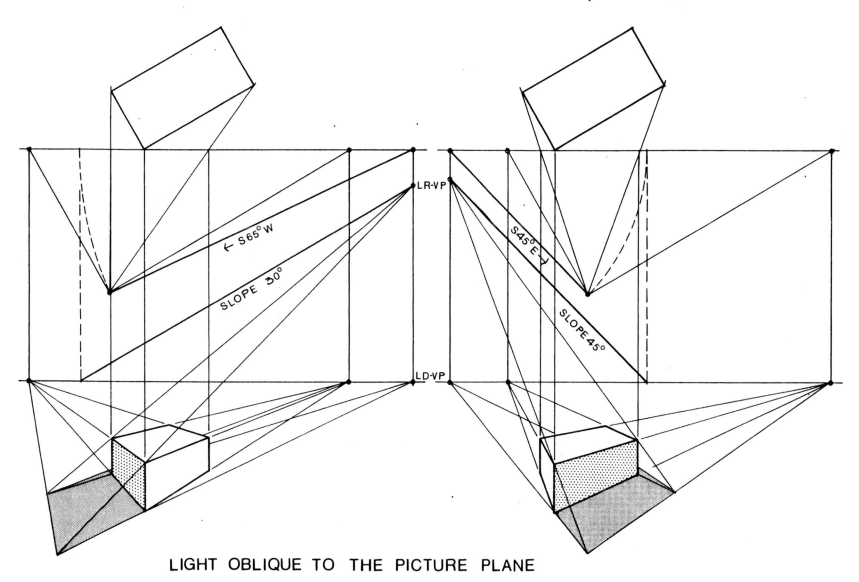

LIGHT OBLIQUE TO THE PICTURE PLANE

CHAPTER 12

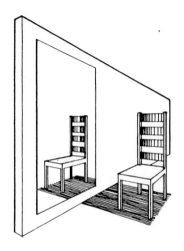

REFLECTIONS

REFLECTIONS

The reflection of an object on a horizontal surface such as a body of water or a shiny surface is an inverted duplicate of the object. The sharpness and clarity of the reflection depends upon the quality of the reflecting surface and lighting conditions. When constructing reflections on horizontal surfaces, two principles need to be considered. (1) The reflected image of a point will lie directly below the actual point. (2) The depth of the reflection will be equal to the height of the object above the reflecting surface. In the examples below, consider the object as resting on a reflecting surface.

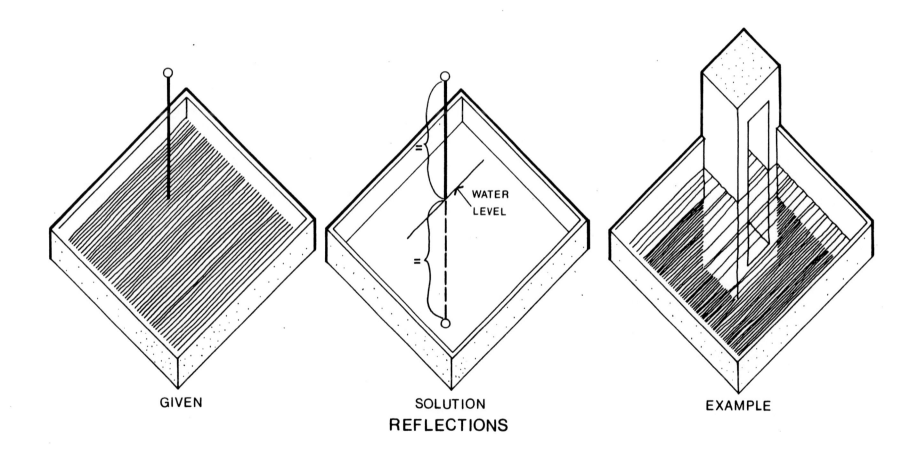

GIVEN   SOLUTION   EXAMPLE

REFLECTIONS

The examples illustrated below are for objects which do not rest on the immediate reflecting surface. In order to find the depth of the reflection in the water, it is first necessary to determine the water level under the parts being reflected.

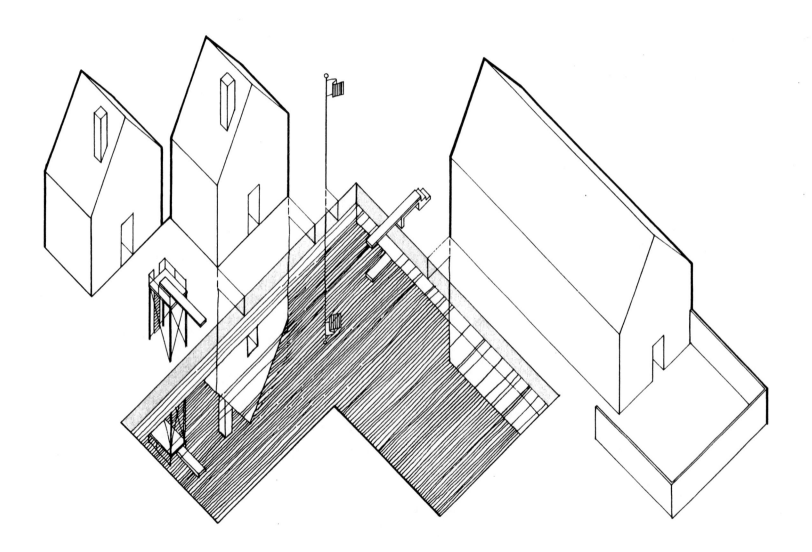

Reflections can also appear on vertical surfaces such as walls and mirrors. Construction of the reflection on a vertical surface is achieved by the use of geometry and the principle that diagonal lines can be used to divide a line or plane in perspective. Below are several examples using this method.

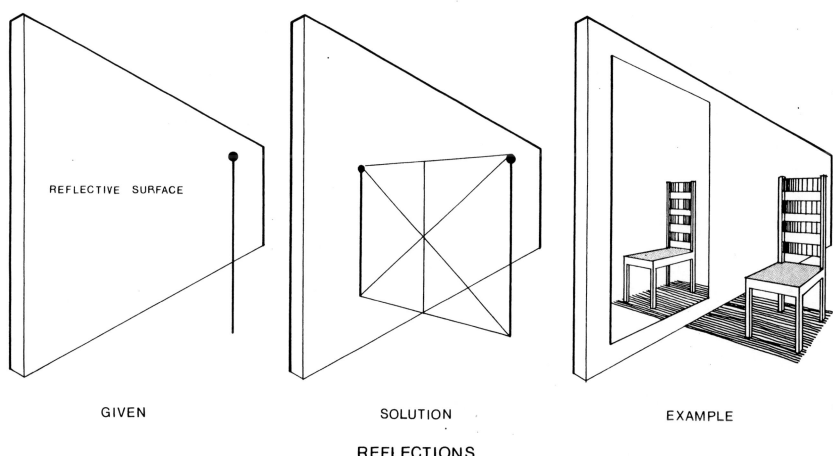

REFLECTIVE   SURFACE

GIVEN   SOLUTION   EXAMPLE

REFLECTIONS

CHAPTER **13**

PRESENTATION DRAWINGS

PRESENTATION DRAWINGS

Presentation drawings are of utmost importance to the student as well as the practicing architect for several reasons. By the nature of the profession we are providing a product which cannot be shown except in drawings or model form. It becomes essential to portray the design clearly to a client, professor, or even to the designer to "preview" or understand the design intent. Presentation drawings differ from other drawing types in respect to communication. Production drawings provide immense amounts of information concerning the construction of a building, but provide no information illustrating the design concept or intent. We must also keep in mind most viewers or clients do not understand complicated production drawings, but can comprehend presentation drawings which communicate in their language. A good design presented poorly will have a lesser chance for acceptance than a poor design presented very well. This chapter deals with constructing drawings that communicate. The principles will apply to all types of drawings. Finally the illustrator must remember the drawings are a means not an end. The finished building is the primary goal and should be the main discussion during a design presentation, not the drawings. If the viewer cannot understand the drawings, then surely he will not understand the design.

Prior to starting any presentation drawing certain principles should be understood and care should be taken not to omit these while planning a drawing.

SHEET ORGANIZATION

The series of lines that form the object is the first step in drawing communication. How these lines are organized with respect to the sheet of drawing field is composition. A well organized drawing will have a certain equilibrium between the two. The easiest way to achieve this is to have the drawing interact with the sheet on a relatively equal basis.

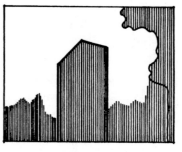

EQUAL

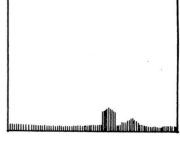

UNBALANCED

PERSPECTIVE PLANES

Perspective drawings exhibit three distinct planes. These are foreground, middle ground and background. Ommission of any of these planes causes a certain amount of disorientation to the viewer. The foreground plane is usually ignored the most, yet is essential in terms of defining where the viewer is in relation to the rest of the building.

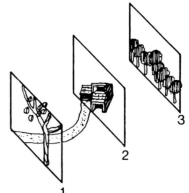

PERSPECTIVE CUES

We all know the phenomena of objects in perspective (i.e., railroad tracks seem to come together, telephone poles are spaced closer as they recede, etc.), yet we forget this applies to material, textures, and other objects. Lines perpendicular to the picture plane (i.e., railroad tracks) diminish to the vanishing point. Lines parallel to the picture plane (i.e., telephone poles) diminish in size and space between each line. Objects of the same size diminish in apparent size as they recede from the viewer. These cues can be used to achieve spatial depth in the drawing.

DRAWING INTENT

Probably the most important idea to keep in mind is "what do I want to communicate with this drawing"? The goal of the drawing should be very clear to you or it will be just a recording of information without the interjection of mood, feeling or intention.

VALUE AND LINE WEIGHT

The value, or lightness or darkness, of a plane or line can instill a visual response portraying depth. A lighter line or plane will tend to recede as compared to the same size line or plane of a darker value. The eye sees objects and forms due to the contrast of the values. In other words, the higher the contrast the easier it is for the eye to "pick up" that form or object. This notion should be utilized when planning a drawing. This becomes especially important when the values occurring in the drawing are more than just pure black and white. Texture on a plane can assign a value to that plane. A brick wall texture indicated by a series of horizontal lines now has a value. The same wall further from the viewer will have the brick lines spaced closer tending to give the plane a darker value. This is an important perspective cue, but does not adhere to the light/recede value phenomena discussed and must be anticipated when constructing drawings with lines as texture. As objects recede a great distance from the viewer, they will become very light in value. This is due to atmospheric conditions (smoke, smog, etc.) and should be incorporated into the drawing when planning values. Therefore, objects closer to the viewer tend to be darker in value than those distant.

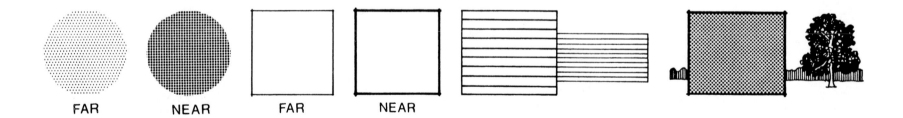

FAR   NEAR   FAR   NEAR

Depth Clues

The purpose of perspective drawing is to give the appearance of depth. As stated earlier this can be achieved by paying attention to the following: (1) Size — Large figures appear closer than smaller figures which appear further away. (2) Amount of Detail — To make an object appear further away reduce the amount of detail. Soft fuzzy lines and shapes appear further away than crisp well defined edges and shapes. (3) Brightness — Closer objects will appear brighter and in full color whereas distant objects will appear greyer in value. Other ways of implying depth in a drawing is to consider organizing the various elements within the composition in the following manner:

1. Overlapping — Objects which overlap will give the appearance of distance because those objects which are partially hidden will appear further away than those in full view. Thus given two objects of the same size, but one overlapping the other, the object in full view will appear near and the other distant.
2. Placement — If an object is placed lower in the composition than others around it the lower object will appear closer. Thus low and high positions can be used to create the feeling of perspective depth.

OVERLAPPING

PLACEMENT

HIERARCHY OF LINE VALUES

The heaviest line weight should profile the form against space. The next line weight should convey a change in plane direction and the lightest weight should indicate texture or something occuring on the plane. Elevation drawings should utilize a series of heavy line weights to profile forms in front of other forms that "cut into space." This will indicate which form is closer to the viewer.

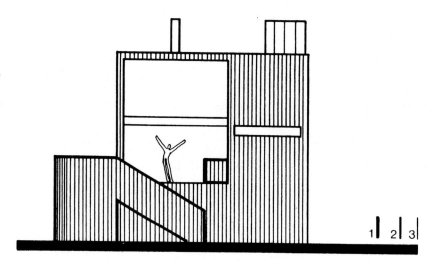

Pictorial drawings used for presentation should utilize the same hierarchy of line values. Heavy lines to profile a shape against space, medium lines for a change in plane direction and light lines to indicate textures or the tonal value of the surface. The three line weights just described were utilized for these drawings. They are: 1 = heavy, 2 = medium, 3 = light.

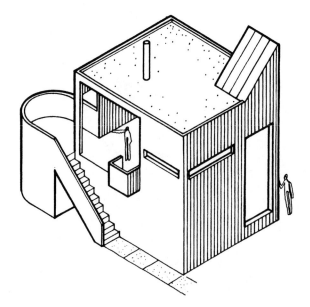

TONAL VALUES

An object can be shown by an outline drawing or line drawing. We perceive the form of that object by the way light strikes its surface and shadows cast by it. Since we live in a world with light, we should understand how light behaves when it strikes a surface directly, indirectly (shade), and the shadow cast by that form.

Tonal values may be indicated by line, lines indicating texture or pure tone. A combination of any of these tones can be utilized. A tone of lines assign a tonal value to each plane. The value of this tone can be increased by spacing the lines closer. The direction of the lines should follow the plane which they are in.

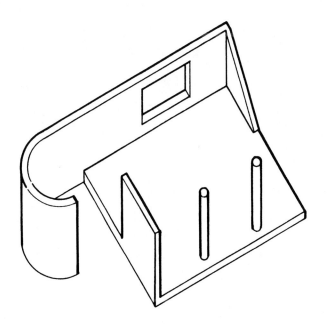
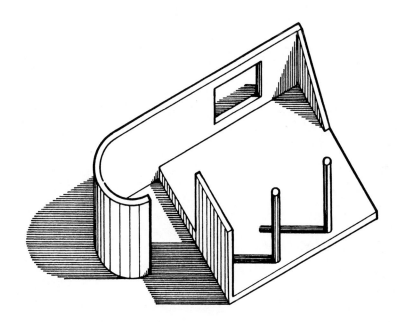

Constructing a drawing utilizing several values of tone must be thought out prior to "rendering" the line drawing. This is essential due to the infinite values possible even though the lines may indicate entirely different textures. It is essential to maintain the contrast between different planes of the building and its environment, entourage etc., and the tonal value will have to be adjusted constantly to achieve this. Contrast of greater degree can provide additional meaning and intent to the drawing. For example, a sphere very light in value against a background dark in value will become the focal point of the drawing.

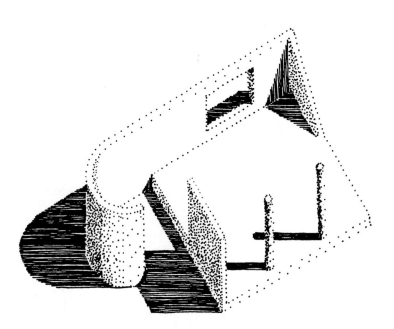

ENTOURAGE

Presentation drawings require simulation of how the building will appear in its context. This will require additional representation of what may occur around it (i.e., people, cars, trees, ground texture, etc.). This will add realism, activity, and scale to the drawing and can also show how the structure may be used.

GROUND TEXTURES

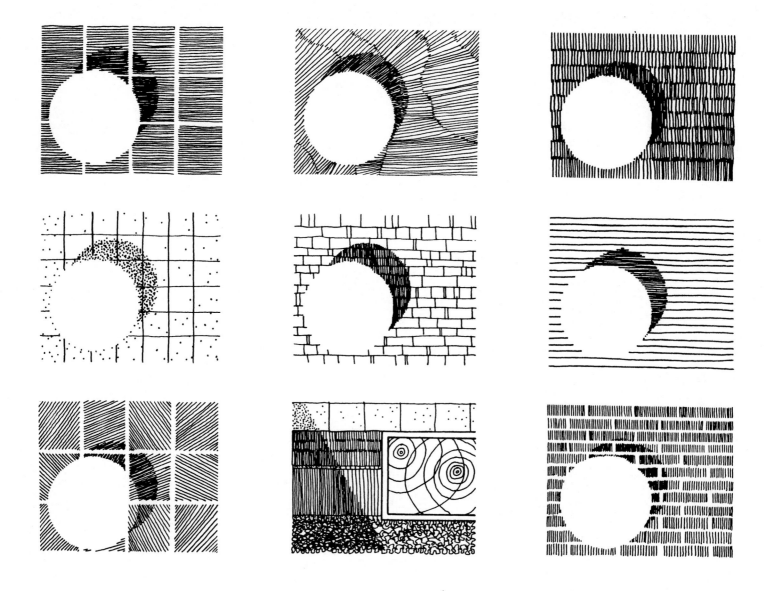

PEOPLE

People should always be included in the presentation drawing for several reasons, to define scale, add activity and show how people may interact with the building, thus illustrating its purpose. It is essential to construct figures proportionally correct. The total height of a person is approximately seven times the head. Once the size is correct, the figure should show activity and be grouped with other figures. Figures in perspectives with an eye level horizon should always be located with their eyes on this line.

AUTOMOBILES

Drawing cars is a matter of constructing a rectangle relative in size to a figure and sub-dividing this into automobile shapes. This is helpful by defining the size of the car regardless of its direction in the drawing. The amount of detail shown may vary from an outline to a well defined car depending on the drawing requirement.

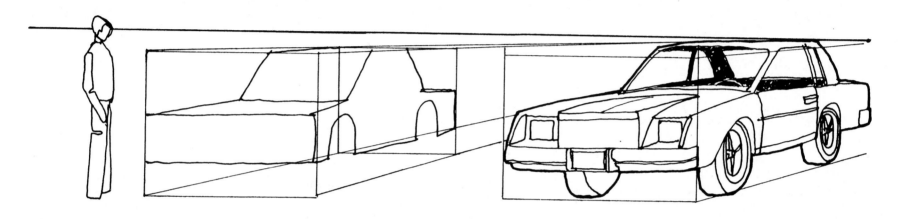

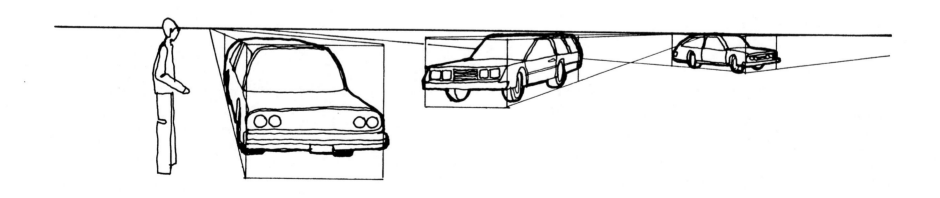

SITE PLAN

The site plan portrays the building in its context. Major elements such as traffic-ways, typography, compass direction, landscape and any other important design determinant should be shown on this drawing. Use of texture can be used to convey ground materials. Shadow should also be shown to illustrate the form and height of the structure and ground plane changes.

FLOOR PLAN

The presentation plan should convey information concerning the arrangement of spaces and the organization to exterior elements. The drawings should eliminate any detail not pertaining to explanation of spatial interrelationships. Providing only this information reinforces the design intent and objectives. Execution of this drawing should provide graphic meaning; i.e., solid walls (solid black lines), passage through walls (door swings), space use (furniture placement). Lighter line weight indicates any texture, object or window.

ONE

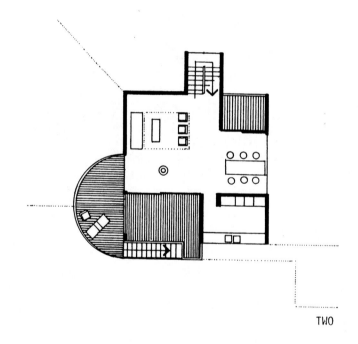

TWO

ELEVATION

As previously discussed in Chapter 6, the elevation conveys the buildings mass, scale, material and context. The penetrations in the wall should be indicated using shade and shadow values. This will also give depth to an otherwise "flat" drawing. The use of a heavy line weight on forms closest to the viewer and medium weights on those receding will also suggest depth. Light lines should be reserved for texture indications.

SECTION

The section conveys interior spatial characteristics such as scale, vertical space relationships, and the penetration of light into the space. It can also show integration of the structure and side conditions. If the site has special qualities, i.e., steep slope, the section can be a powerful communicative drawing illustrating the design intent. The execution of a section is much like the plan. Any solid element that is cut, such as a wall or floor, should be portrayed as a dark solid line of heavy weight. Changes of plane and texture should utilize lighter line weights.

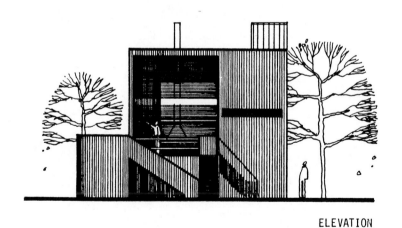

ELEVATION

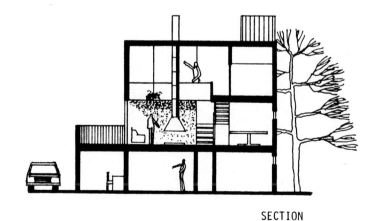

SECTION

PERSPECTIVE

Perspective drawings provide the most realistic representation of the building. The two types generally used are eye level or aerial. Eye level drawings convey a view we will actually experience; whereas an aerial view can include more information such as a large complex structure or the environment adjacent to it. The decision as to which type of perspective to use depends on what information must be communicated. The execution of these drawings will be discussed in the following section, component by component. The general concepts of drawing organization will be presented in a manner to provide the student with guidelines to build drawings. They provide our main objective . . . communication.

EYE LEVEL

AERIAL

PRESENTATION PACKAGE

Executing a presentation involves the following:

A set of drawings which convey information about the total project.

1. Site plan to illustrate the building's environment and how the building responds to it, i.e., view, existing buildings, sun orientation, wind direction, topography, traffic circulation and other siting determinants.
2. A plan showing the relationship of internal spaces illustrating how it fulfills user's need as well as how it responds to site conditions.
3. A building section to show the relationship of vertical space.
4. Elevation drawings to illustrate the building's external configuration.
5. A perspective or paraline drawing to show the total integration of the different elements of the building.
6. A model to show the three dimensional aspects of the form of the building.

A combination of any of these will suffice depending on the complexity of the building and the client's knowledge and education.

It is imperative these drawings be complete, coherent and consistent, consistent in size, orientation and technique.

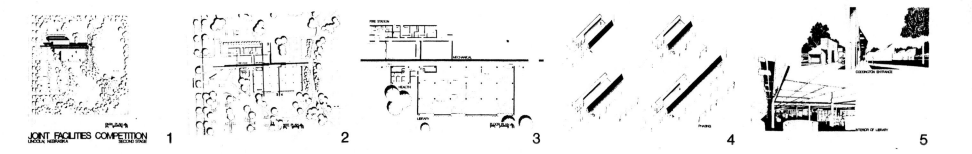

JOINT FACILITIES COMPETITION   1   2   3   4   5

PRESENTATION DRAWING CONSTRUCTION

DRAWING INTENT

The concept of the building consists of the large masonry wall which separates the entirely different functions housed within the structure. It serves as a heat storage wall as well as reflecting the internal circulation spine and entrance. It quickly becomes apparent these conceptual ideas should be utilized for determining the vantage point of the drawing. Several overlays should be used to achieve exact view desired.

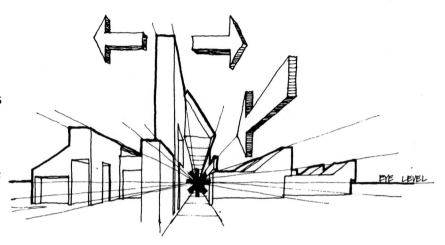

ENTOURAGE PLACEMENT

Following construction of the rough perspective layout, an overlay consisting of tree, figure and auto locations can be shown in relation to the building. Avoid locating trees in critical information areas such as corners of planes or exact center of drawing. Trees should be additional information and should never "take over" the composition. At this point a decision should be made concerning the composition of the drawing. The drawing should be in equilibrium, a balance between the lines forming the object and the white space left over.

VALUE DECISIONS

At this point, an overlay investigating the tonal values of the drawing should be constructed. It will allow an abstract view of light/dark value relationship in the final drawing. This step is imperative and should not be deleted. At this stage, the values can be adjusted to achieve the contrast required to show form of the building and its relationship to the environment. Several studies must be made to achieve this critical component of the drawing.

DRAWING EXECUTION

The final step is indicating materials, textures, and the way light effects the form. The interaction of people with the building gives not only scale, but also an indication of how the structure may be used. Entourage also gives scale, but more important indicates how the structure is integrated with the environment. If the preceding step, involving the value study was adhered to, the addition of material rendition should be successful irregardless of the medium utilized. Pencil, ink, or color requires the same process of decision making.

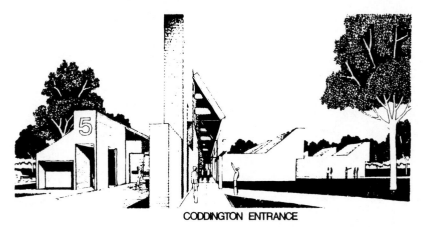

CODDINGTON ENTRANCE

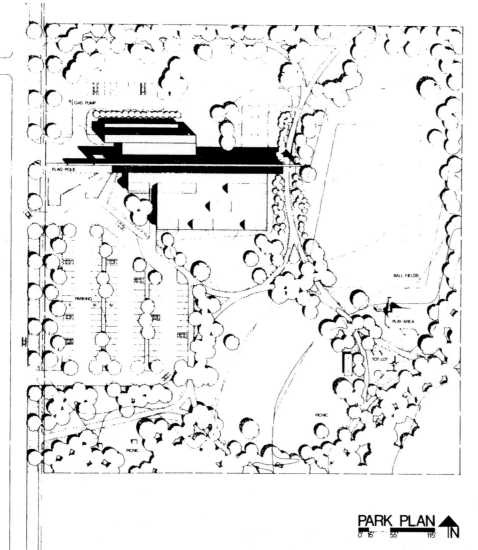

PARK PLAN
0' 15'   55'   115'

JOINT FACILITIES COMPETITION
LINCOLN, NEBRASKA   SECOND STAGE

1

A PRESENTATION DRAWING PACKAGE

Illustrated on the next five pages are examples of a set of presentation drawings done by the architectural firm of The Clark Enersen Partners, Lincoln, Nebraska. These second stage drawings were submitted in a competition for a combined joint facilities of health, fire station, and library. The design was awarded first place by the jury which judged the competition.

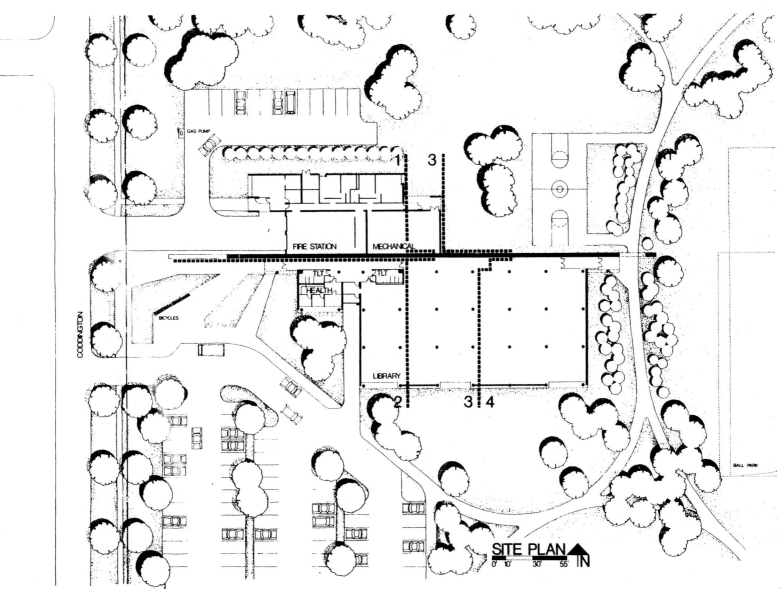

GAS PUMP

1   3

FIRE STATION   MECHANICAL

CODDINGTON

TLT   TLT

HEALTH

BICYCLES

LIBRARY

2   3 4

BALL PARK

SITE PLAN
0' 10'   30' 55'   N

2

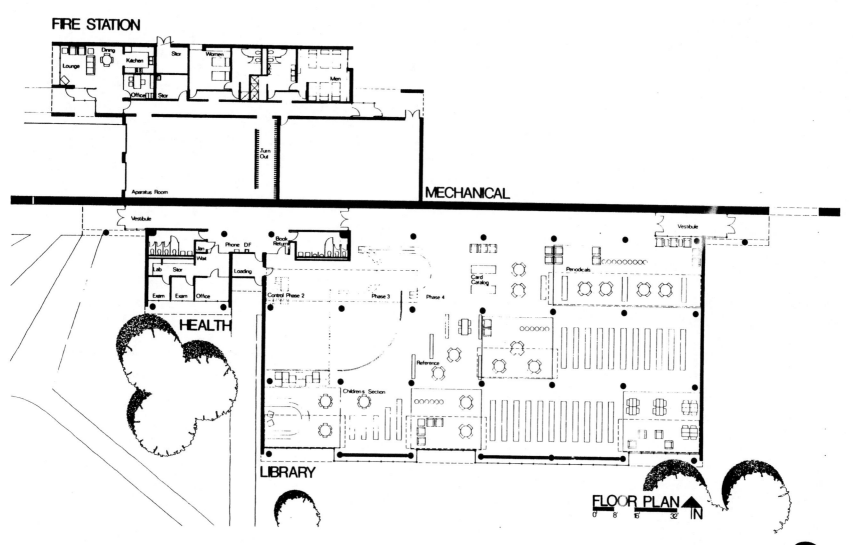

FIRE STATION

MECHANICAL

HEALTH

LIBRARY

FLOOR PLAN
0 8' 16'   32'   IN

3

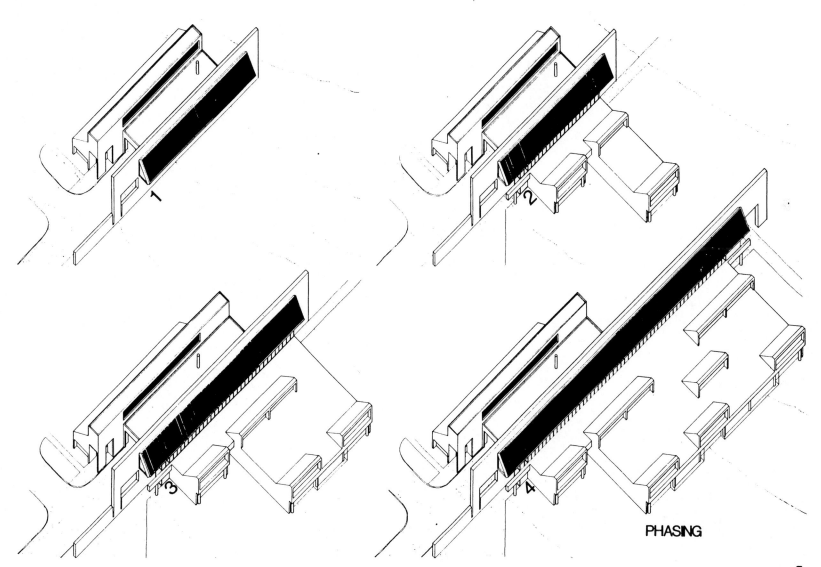

PHASING

4

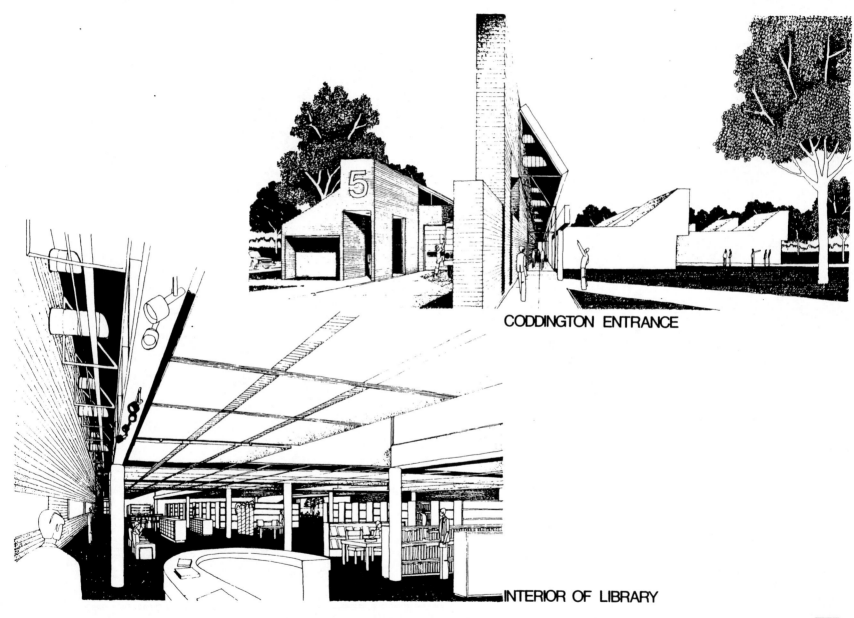

CODDINGTON ENTRANCE

INTERIOR OF LIBRARY

5

FINAL PRESENTATION DRAWING CONSIDERATIONS

As previously mentioned, attempting a design presentation requires consideration of a variety of different concerns, from drawing intent to the finished rendering. Listed below are some important considerations which should be addressed before the final presentation is begun.

1. Format—Most design presentations are either done on some type of illustration board, sheets of paper, or ozalid prints so that they can be viewed by a class or reviewed by a jury. It is very important that the size and shape of these drawings be considered before starting on the final since it is desirable to achieve maximum communication and impact. Board placement and arrangement will dictate how the design is perceived and communicated. The information presented should flow in a logical sequence from drawing to drawing and board to board. This sequence of information should provide the observer with a quick understanding of the problem and its solution with a minimum of intense investigation. Errors in drawing, labeling, and dimensioning reduces the impact of the solution and generally suggests an offhand approach to the problem. Such errors should be avoided at all cost if the design and designer wish to maintain high creditability with the observer.

The organization of subject matter in the presentation should allow the observer to progress from the general to the specific while viewing the drawings. Relationships developed in plan should be easily understood in elevation/section, and visualized in pictorial/perspective so that significant details will be meaningful and relevant. Thus it is important that a systematic arrangement of data be considered so that the entire collection of material forms a package which communicates the solution to its fullest.

2. Composition—Often when a number of boards are used together as a package, it is helpful to have some organizing device such as a title strip, border, or logo which can "tie" the boards together as a unit. It is important all the boards or sheets be of the same size and placed in the same direction, and especially have the same format so that the entire collection of drawings has a professional appearance. Boards of different size, texture, color and format tend to be confusing and reduces communication.

3. Drawing Techniques—Every attempt should be made to use the best skills and techniques available for the final presentation. As a student, it is often difficult to develop a highly professional skill in a specific rendering medium because one is always learning and practicing these skills in school. One approach to developing a use of mediums is to experiment using different techniques on daily problems and exercises given in rendering and presentation classes. After developing some basic skills, these can be used on design presentations until others have been practiced.

Most students tend to have greater success when beginning with simple pencil or ink drawings. These can be high lighted with felt tip pens, watercolor, pastel, and colored pencil. One should not attempt to do a full color rendering of a presentation until some fundamental techniques have been developed. Too often students will overwork their drawings in an attempt to create a professional look. Overworking either the drawing or the color reduces the freshness of the presentation. Some of the most successful drawings are simple line drawings with small selected amounts of color added for accent or emphasis.

4. Materials and Supplies—It is important to have the proper equipment and supplies available when attempting a set of presentation drawings. Listed below are a variety of items that are suggested for use in presentation drawings.

General Materials:

- Drafting equipment
- Pencils
- Technical pens for inking
- Erasers
- T-square
- Triangles
- Scales

Miscellaneous:

- Rubber cement
- Drafting tape
- Exacto knife
- Templates
- French curves

Color Materials:

- Select a color medium of your choice and papers and equipment appropriate for the medium

Water Color or Tempera:

- Paints in the tube
- Watercolor brushes (Ox hair or red sable)
- Mixing trays or a plate
- Water containers
- Organic sponge
- Watercolor paper or boards

Color Pencils:

A good set of Color pencils that give a wide range of colors
Kneeded eraser
Soft pencil eraser
Good quality drawing paper

Pastels:

A good set of pastels
Kneeded eraser
Several smudge sticks or stumps
Razor blade or Exacto knife
Kleenex
Fixative
Charcoal paper

Felt tip or Markers:

As complete a set of markers as you can afford. The set should include primary and secondary colors, a series of grays, and a variety of earth tones, brown through green.
A rag paper made specifically for use with markers is desirable, but a variety of papers can be used.

PRESENTATION DRAWING EXAMPLES

The following drawings are examples of student work courtesy of the College of Architecture, the University of Nebraska. Each problem illustrates a variety of presentation, techniques, styles, and format. They range from the precise technical drawing of the International House, to the freehand style used on the rendering of the kitchen. Note how all drawings are linked together by either format, sheet size, layout, and rendering style so that it is easy to identify that they belong to one another in a group arrangement.

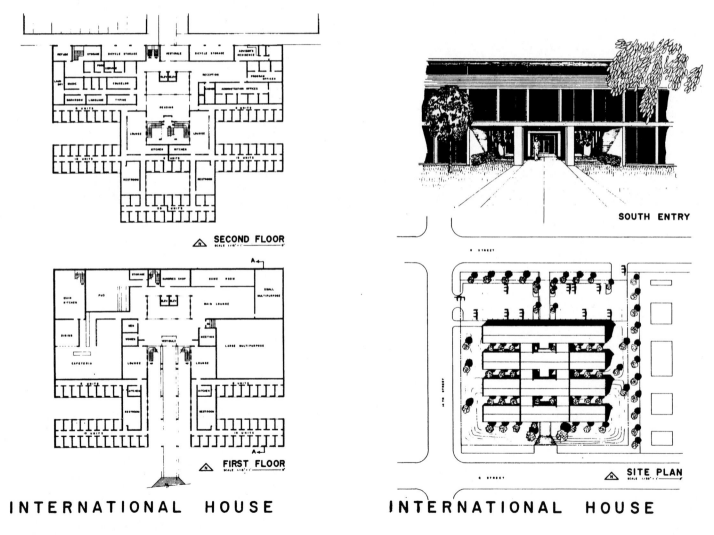

INTERNATIONAL HOUSE   INTERNATIONAL HOUSE

SECTION THRU A-A
SCALE 1/16"=1'   0'

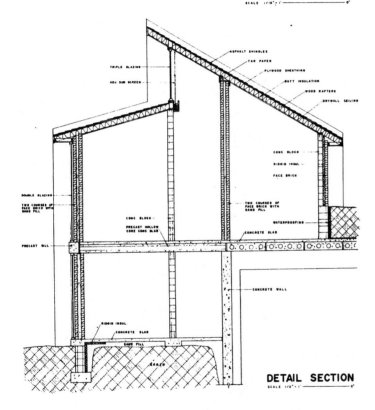

DETAIL SECTION
SCALE 1/2"=1'   0'

INTERNATIONAL HOUSE

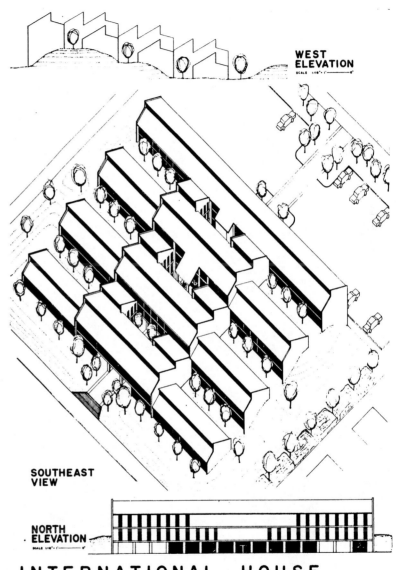

WEST ELEVATION
SCALE 1/16"=1'   0'

SOUTHEAST VIEW

NORTH ELEVATION
SCALE 1/16"=1'   0'

INTERNATIONAL HOUSE

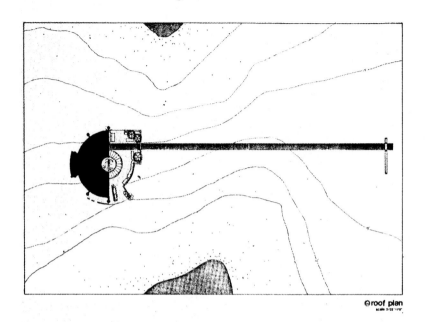

east elevation

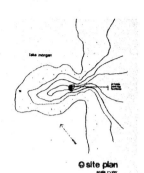

site plan
scale 1"=100'

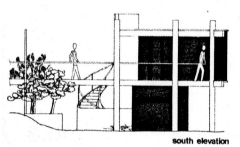

south elevation

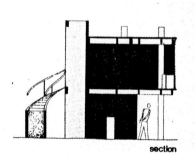

section

roof plan
scale 3/32"=1'0"

A JUDGE'S PAVILION
DESIGN 345
T. WETHERILT   scale 1/4"=1'0"

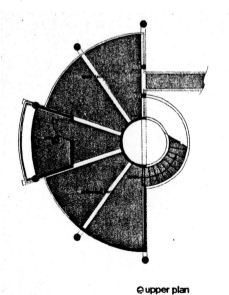

upper plan

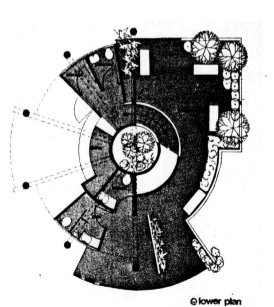

lower plan

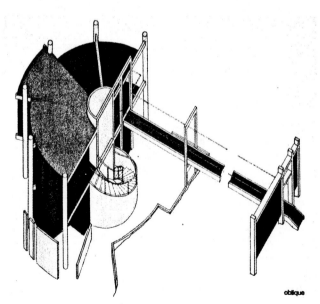

oblique

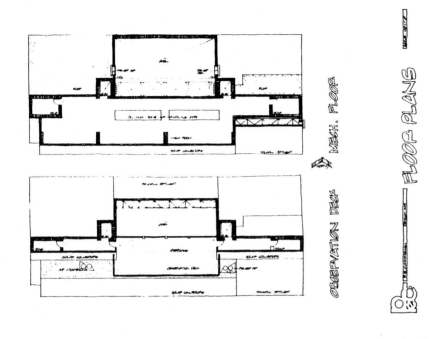

MECH. FLOOR

OBSERVATION DECK

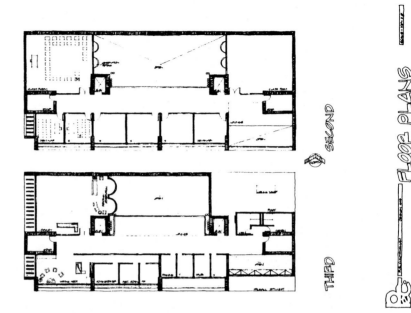

FLOOR PLANS

SECOND

THIRD

FLOOR PLANS

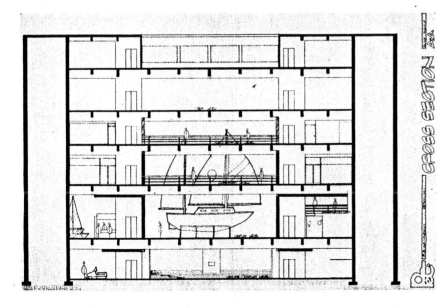

CROSS SECTION

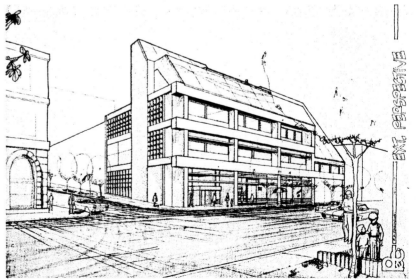

EXT. PERSPECTIVE

WALL SECTION 1.

INT. PERSPECTIVE

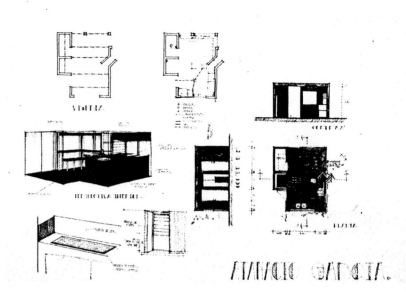

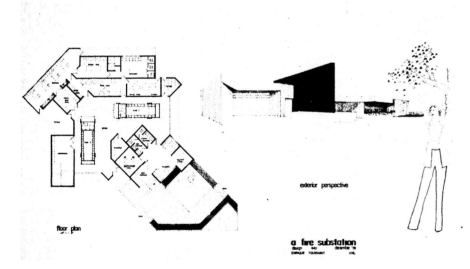

floor plan

exterior perspective

a fire substation

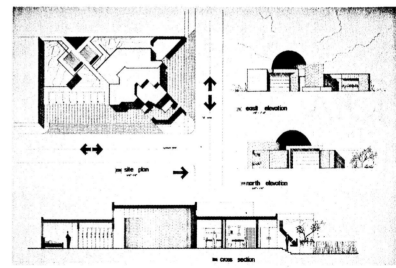

east elevation

site plan

north elevation

cross section

CHAPTER **14**

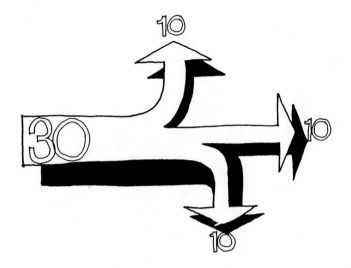

DIAGRAMMING

DIAGRAMMING

Architects are known for their ability to draw representations of a building. In reality a tremendous amount of thought, problem solving, scribbles and sketches representing the thought process precede the finished design. These drawings are diagrams. Diagrams allow us to *think* in visual terms. Complexity in today's buildings bring out all kinds of supportive data, (i.e., user-need surveys, life cycle costing, traffic analysis, projected space demand, etc.,) which are useful, but do not help us "see" the true basis of the problem. Diagramming allows us to evaluate a problem by providing an abstract visual representation which is open to several interpretations and manipulations. This provides a means to visually "think out" and explore possible solutions that we and others can understand.

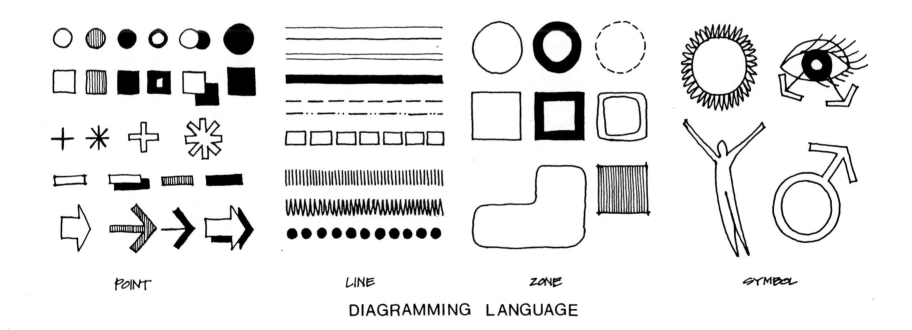

POINT   LINE   ZONE   SYMBOL

DIAGRAMMING   LANGUAGE

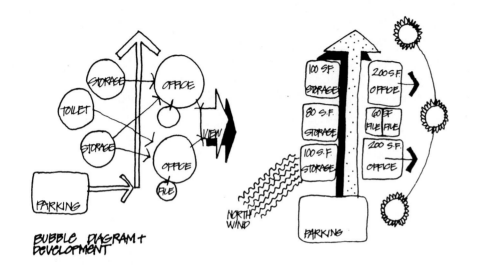

BUBBLE DIAGRAM +
DEVELOPMENT

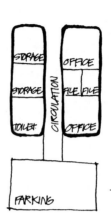

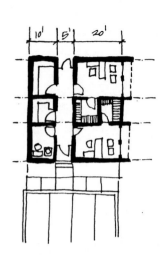

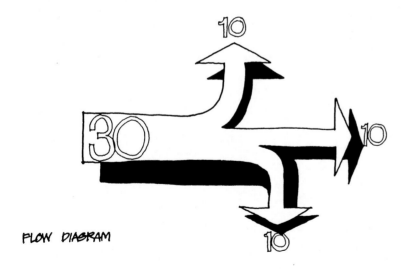

PLOW DIAGRAM

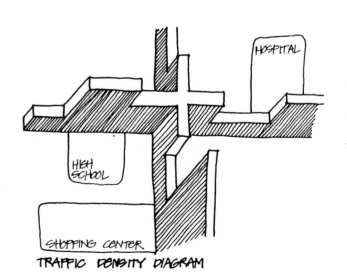

TRAFFIC DENSITY DIAGRAM

PROGRAM STATEMENT:

A library where book theft has been a problem. It is desirable for one observer to see all the book stacks.

PROGRAM STATEMENT:

Site on a campus was quite frequently cut across by pedestrian lines of desire.

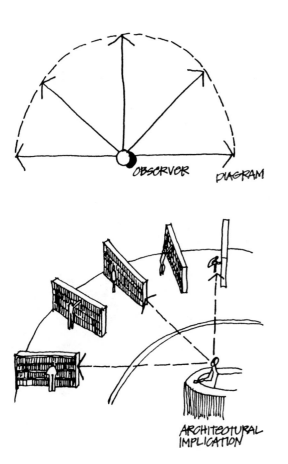

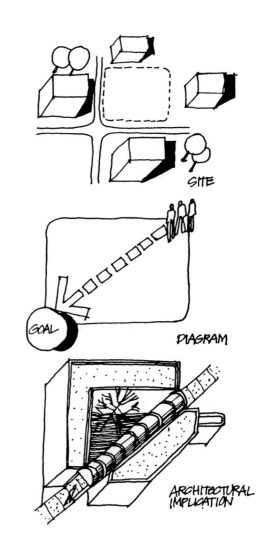

FACTOR ANALYSIS:

Evaluating complex situations graphically through the use of a series of information overlays provides a visual solution not evident by analyzing a single factor. This method can be utilized for any number of factors affecting the project.

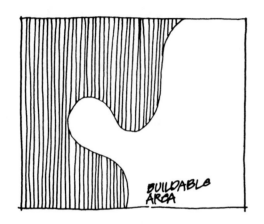

BUILDABLE AREA

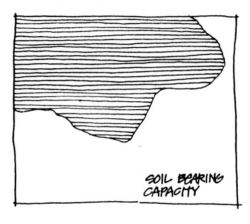

SOIL BEARING CAPACITY

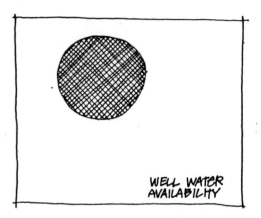

WELL WATER AVAILABILITY

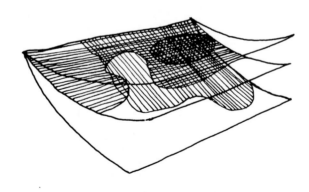

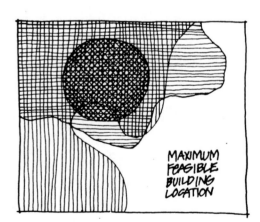

MAXIMUM FEASIBLE BUILDING LOCATION

DIAGRAM DEVELOPMENT

A diagram can progress from abstract terms to a well defined plan.

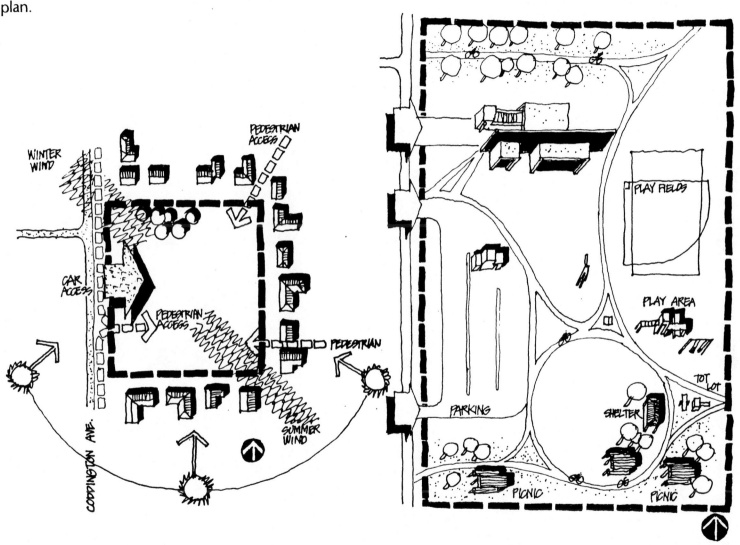

DIAGRAM DEVELOPMENT

The following three pages illustrate the development of a diagram from the given data and initial information to the completed solution. Adding color will aid in the visualization of the analysis and diagrams.

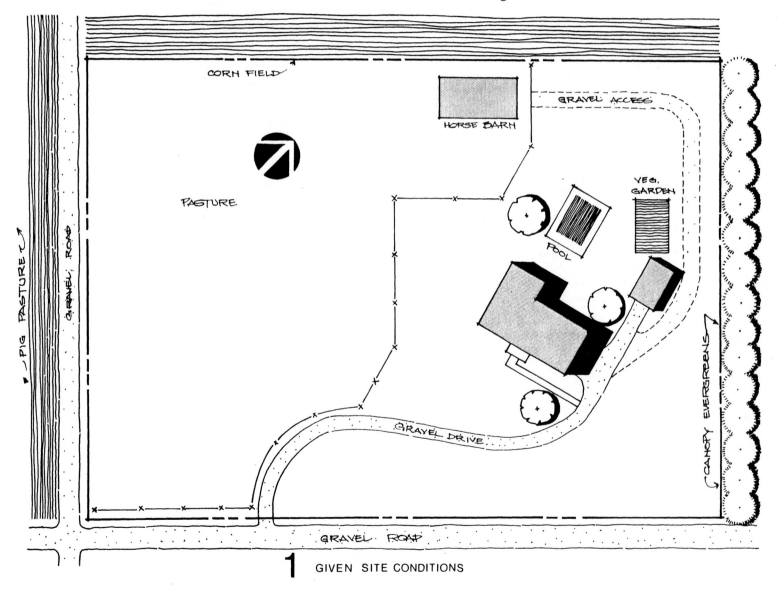

1 GIVEN SITE CONDITIONS

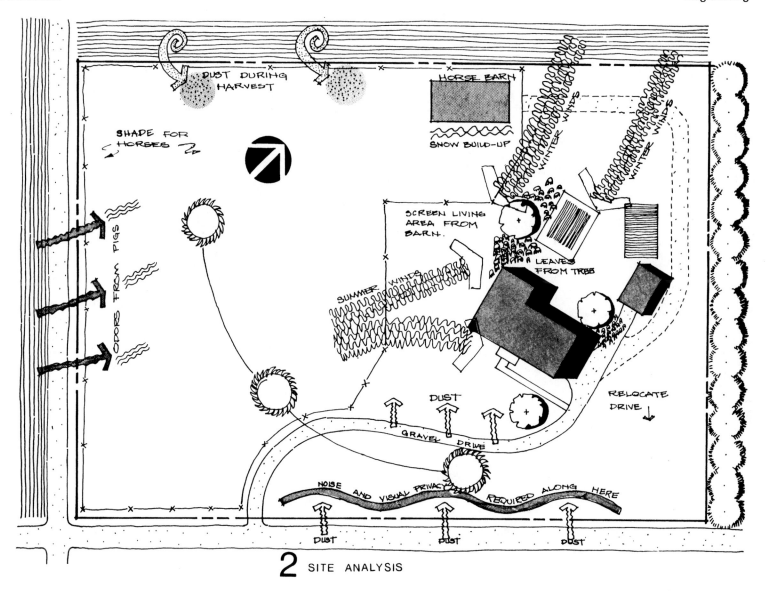

DUST DURING
HARVEST

HORSE BARN

SNOW BUILD-UP

SHADE FOR
HORSES

ODORS FROM PIGS

SCREEN LIVING
AREA FROM
BARN.

WINTER WINDS

WINTER WINDS

LEAVES
FROM TREE

SUMMER WINDS

DUST

RELOCATE
DRIVE

GRAVEL DRIVE

NOISE AND VISUAL PRIVACY   REQUIRED ALONG HERE

DUST   DUST   DUST

2 SITE ANALYSIS

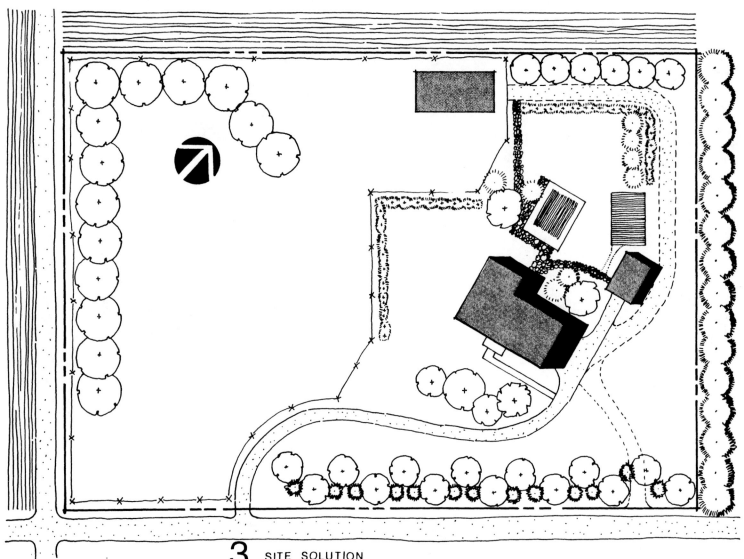

3 SITE SOLUTION

REVIEW QUESTIONS

CHAPTER 1—LETTERING

1. What are three compositional elements of balance with respect to lettering?
2. Space between letters in a word is very important when lettering. This space is achieved by keeping the net (distance, area, proportion) between letters equal.
3. When spacing words in a sentence, it is best to keep the space between words equal to the (area, width, height) of the letters used.
4. The understood denominator on the Ames Lettering Guide is _____ .
5. What is a serif? Give an example of where it is used in lettering.
6. Using the number 8 on the Ames Lettering Guide will produce guidelines _____ inches tall.
7. Should guidelines for lettering be left on the paper or erased?
8. What is more important, lettering style or readability?
9. Is it better to be consistent in the use of upper case letters or should one combine alphabets when lettering?
10. What value of lead is good for lettering?

CHAPTER 2—BASIC DRAWING EQUIPMENT

1. What is the basic difference between standard drawing pencils and micro.drawing pencils? What advantage do they have over wooden pencils?
2. Drawing leads are graded according to hardness. Rank the following leads in order of hardness starting from soft to hard. The leads are: H, 3H, B, F, HB.
3. What group of leads are used to darken in a finished drawing?
4. What leads are used for layout and guide lines?
5. On what side of the drafting table is the T-square placed for a right-handed person?
6. Using the 30°–60° and 45° triangles together, what are the possible angles one can obtain from horizontal?
7. What advantage does an adjustable triangle have over standard triangles?
8. How many scales does the triangular architects scale have?
9. Which line is darker in value, cutting-plane or centerline?
10. Which of the following lines is longer? 2'-6" @ 1"=1'-0", 4'-0" @ 3/4"=1'-0", or 9'-0" @ ¼"=1'-0".
11. What scale on the architects scale would you choose to make drawings that are full size?

12. The value of one millimetre is approximately that of a pencil line but in fact equals what width in metric?
13. How does the scale notation of the Engineer's scale differ from the Architect's?
14. What metric scale is similar to the foot/inch scale of 3″=1′-0″?
15. Following border lines, what type of line is next darkest and boldest?

CHAPTER 3—ORTHOGRAPHIC PROJECTION

1. In orthographic projection, the image of the object is projected on a set of picture planes which are _____ degrees to each other.
2. Name the three principal planes of projection.
3. What is a "hinge line"? How is it used?
4. What are auxiliary views used for?
5. Name three types of auxiliary views?
6. Given the following, plot point "A" in all three views.

   Point "A" lies: On "H"
                    ½″ left of "P"
                    ¼″ behind "F"

7. Given point "B", what are its coordinate distances from H, F, P?

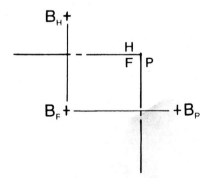

8. Draw any auxiliary inclined view of point "B" in problem #7.
9. Sketch the H and F views of any line that meets the following requirements: Classification = Horizontal
                                                                                    Bearing is S 30° E
                                                                                    In what view is the line true length?

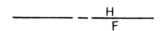

10. Draw the H and F views of any line that would be classified as oblique.

11. An auxiliary elevation view is always projected off of the _____ view.
12. An auxiliary inclined view is always projected off of either the (horizontal, frontal, profile) views. Underline correct choice.
13. Is it possible for an oblique line to be true length in either the H or F views?
14. Is the following statement true? The slope angle of a line can only be measured where the line appears in true length in an elevation view.
15. An auxiliary elevation view is any auxiliary view which shows the (frontal, horizontal, profile) plane as an edge.
16. Bearing of a line is always measured in what view?
17. When looking at the front view, the H/F hinge line represents the (horizontal, frontal, profile) plane as an edge.
18. Is a line classified as oblique ever parallel to the principal reference planes?

19. When measuring the bearing of a line, the angle will always be (acute, obtuse).
20. What is the difference between slope angle of a line and slope of a line?
21. Name four ways to graphically represent a plane.
22. In order to measure the inclination of a plane, the plane must be seen as an _____ in any elevation view.
23. Is it possible to measure the inclination of a plane in an auxiliary inclined view? Why?
24. Find the inclination and true size of the plane shown below.

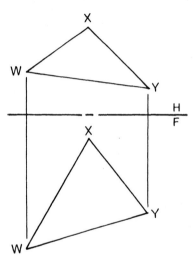

25. In order to find the dihedral angle between two planes the line of intersection must be seen as a _____ .
26. The dihedral angle formed between two planes shows the planes as _____ .
27. Given the two intersecting planes, determine their dihedral angle.

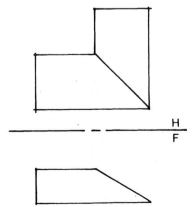

28. When finding the angle between a line and a plane, the final view of line and plane should show the plane as an
_____ and the line in _____ .
29. Any view projected off the true size view of a plane will show the plane as an _____ .
30. Name three methods for determining the piercing point of a line and plane.
31. Locate where the line pierces the plane.

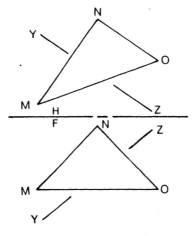

32. Name two methods for finding the line of intersection between planes.
33. Find the line of intersection between the two planes.

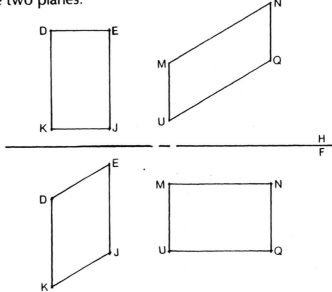

CHAPTER 4—PROBLEM SOLUTIONS BY ROTATION

1. When is rotation used over auxiliary views?
2. When using rotation to solve problems, an axis of rotation must be identified and seen as a _____ before the object is rotated. .
3. Using rotation only, determine the true length of the line.

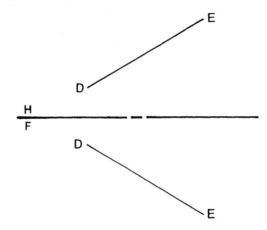

4. Using rotation, find a point view of the line.

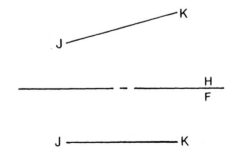

5. Given the H and F views of a line, determine its slope angle using rotation.

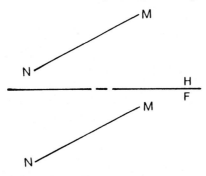

6. Using rotation, locate a point view of the given line.

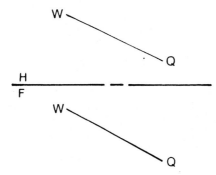

7. Using rotation, find the true size of the given plane.

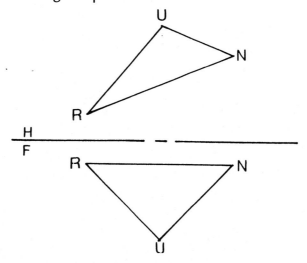

8. Determine the inclination of the plane using rotation.

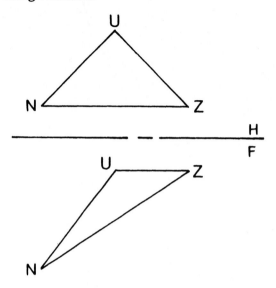

CHAPTER 5—PROJECTION OF SOLIDS

1. When drawing an object, which type of lines take precedence over centerlines?
2. Given the H and F views of an object, draw as many right profile views as possible. Do not alter the given views.

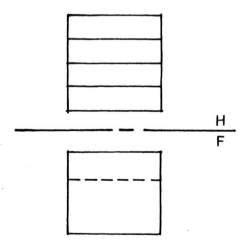

3. Draw as many possible right side views of the given object as possible. Do not alter the given H and F views.

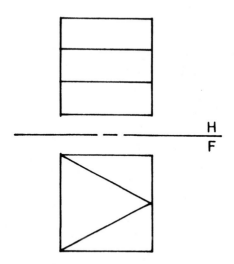

4. Given the front and right profile views, complete the plan view.

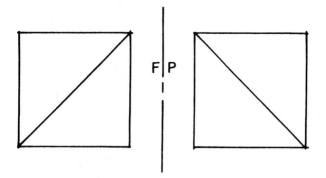

CHAPTER 6—DRAWING CONVENTIONS

1. What is the purpose of using presentation drawings?
2. Who is the principle user of production drawings?
3. List six items that a set of production drawings might include.
4. Describe how a set of presentation drawings might be used.
5. In what manner are production drawings duplicated?
6. How is the type of drawing influenced by its use? For example, how will the style of a drawing vary with respect to usage?
7. List items which might appear on a site plan.
8. Often the site plan is drawn using the engineer's scale. Can you give a reason for this?
9. The floor plan is actually a _____ section placed high enough to locate all openings in plan.
10. What is the purpose of a floor plan?
11. Sketch 3 different ways to render the walls of a floor plan.
12. What is the purpose of an elevation in architecture?
13. Elevations are (1, 2, 3) dimensional. Choose best answer.
14. What does the term "out of projection" mean when drawing elevations?
15. Why would an architect use section drawings to explain a building?
16. Draw a typical cutting-plane line.
17. Why are symbol indications used in sectional drawings?
18. What distinguishes a transverse section from a longitudinal section?
19. What is the advantage of using a half section?
20. Distinguish between a design section and a structural section.
21. Give an example where a detailed section would be useful.
22. Where are typical wall sections taken in a building?
23. What is another name for section-lining?
24. The symbol for wood has two types of drawings, explain why this takes place and its usage.
25. Dimensions on plans are composed of two types, either overall or intermediate. Describe their differences.
26. Name several conventions of architectural dimensioning.
27. Describe the basic theory of masonry and wood frame dimensioning.
28. When dimensioning, arrowheads or slash marks are often used on dimensional lines, if dots are used what do they indicate?
29. Are door swings and the width of doors dimensioned on a plan if they occur in the center of the scheme?
30. Where are the overall dimensions on a wood frame construction located?

CHAPTER 7 — GEOMETRY IN ARCHITECTURE

1. What is a generatrix? Give an example of where it is used.
2. Name a single-curved surface.
3. Is a single-curved surfaced developable?
4. If a warped surface is made up of straight lines, why is it classified as nondevelopable?
5. Name 4 double-curved surfaces.
6. What is the difference between a right cone and a oblique cone?
7. What is a helix and how is it useful in architecture?
8. Name three conic sections.
9. How does a conoid differ from a cylindroid?
10. In what manner does a paraboloid differ from a hyperboloid?
11. Name four double-curved surfaces and sketch an example of each.
12. Name those surfaces which can be developed exactly and those which can be approximated.
13. What is a directrix and how is it used?
14. Explain how a hyperboloid of revolution is generated.
15. When determining the line of intersection between different solids, it is important to use the proper cutting-plane to aid in finding the intersection. Sketch a cylinder, cone, and sphere and illustrate various positions of cutting-planes and their resultant lines of intersections.
16. If a right cone and a right cylinder intersect, what type of cutting-plane is most useful in determining their line of intersection?
17. A horizontal cutting-plane placed parallel to the base of a right cone will produce what type of line of intersection on the cone?
18. Generally, when finding the line of intersection between solids, vertical and horizontal cutting-planes are used. Why is this?
19. Give the equation for a simple parabola. Sketch a grid and using your equation illustrate how a parabola is drawn.
20. Draw the major diameter of a circle equal to 2 inches. Draw the minor diameter equal to 1 inch. Using the cutting-plane method, establish enough points on the curve to draw an ellipse.

CHAPTER 8 — PICTORIAL DRAWING — AXONOMETRIC AND OBLIQUE

1. When are pictorial drawings used?
2. What does the term "pictorial drawing" refer to?
3. Name the 3 types of pictorial drawings often used in architecture.
4. Can axonometric projection be derived through the system of orthographic projection?

5. What types of drawings are included in axonometric?
6. Distinguish between axonometric projection and drawing. Which of the types is larger? Why?
7. How does isometric projection differ from dimetric projection?
8. When would one choose isometric over dimetric?
9. In what manner does trimetric differ from isometric and diametric?
10. Name the three position for the axes in isometric.
11. What is a non-isometric line? Why is it so important in pictorial drawing?
12. Show the various steps necessary to construct a four-centered ellipse.
13. Illustrate three positions for dimetric and the scale ratios used.
14. When would a sectional dimetric be used over a normal exterior dimetric of a building?
15. Can oblique drawing be obtained through the use of orthographic projection? Why?
16. Name three types of oblique drawings and their scale ratios.
17. What angle is oblique elevational drawings use for projecting depth in the drawing?
18. Why would you choose elevational oblique over isometric?
19. At what angle is plan oblique drawn?
20. Will circles appear as circles or ellipses in plan oblique if placed on the roof of a flat roof building?

CHAPTER 9—PERSPECTIVE

1. Why is perspective the most natural appearing type of pictorial?
2. With respect to perspective nomenclature, what is the sight point? What does it actually represent in perspective theory?
3. The intersection of the ground plane and the picture plane produce the _____ .
4. Describe the concept of vanishing point.
5. Name three perspective types. How do they differ?
6. The height of the observer in relation to the ground plane determines the location of the horizon line and in turn determines if the view will be from _____ .
7. For a normal view, how far above the ground line should the horizon be placed?
8. What does moving the picture plane closer to the sight point do to the perspective image?
9. What angle is used for the cone of vision in two point perspective?
10. Why use a cone of vision?
11. How does the common or office method for drawing a perspective differ from using the perspective plan method?
12. Explain the importance of placing the object next to the picture plane in plan when laying out a perspective.
13. What does the family of lines refer to when drawing a perspective?
14. Vanishing traces are used in what manner in perspective?

15. How does parallel perspective differ from angular perspective?
16. What is the cone of vision angle for parallel perspective?
17. Describe how the left and right measuring points are found in angular perspective.
18. Can the measuring point system be used for one-point perspective construction?
19. Why is three point perspective the least used of the various types of perspective types?
20. Where would the horizon be placed in order to have a view looking up from the bottom in perspective?

Chapter 10—Perspective Sketching

1. What is the key to using the method of perspective sketching as developed by William Kirby Lockard?
2. Since the system of perspective sketching as outlined in Chapter 10 is a combination of geometrical and human judgment, should it be used only in initial conceptial sketches? Why?
3. What is the height of the basic frame in perspective sketching?
4. How are the 10 foot widths established?
5. Probably the most important step in perspective sketching is locating 10 foot depths. Explain how this is done.
6. Using the Lockard method, sketch a space which is 15 feet wide, 10 feet high, and 12 feet deep. Locate a skylight in the center of the space which is 3 feet square. Leave in construction lines but darken in outlines.
7. Can Lockards method be used for exterior perspective?
8. Explain how to vary the size of the perspective sketch to make it larger or smaller?
9. Using the method of perspective sketching as described in Chapter 10, where is the least distortion occur? Why?
10. If only one vanishing point is located on the paper in the perspective sketch, where is the other vanishing point located?

Chapter 11—Shades and Shadows—Orthographic and Perspective

1. Describe the standard light ray and its use in casting shadows.
2. List the two principles that are used the most when casting light rays.
3. How do you determine the difference between shade and shadow in a drawing?
4. When casting shadows in orthographic the problem can often be reduced to finding where a line (light ray) pierces a plane. Illustrate this principle with simple sketches.
5. Draw a set of stairs in orthographic and cast the shadows on the stairs using the standard light ray angle.
6. Name and illustrate the two fundamental principles of casting shades and shadows in perspective.
7. What is the key to casting shadows of an overhang on a building?

8. Why and when would you choose to use a light ray that is oblique to the picture plane?
9. What do the terms LD-VP and LR-VP mean with respect to casting shades and shadows with oblique light rays?
10. If the direction of light has a bearing of south, the LR-VP will be located _____ the horizon.

CHAPTER 12—REFLECTIONS

1. The reflection of an object on a horizontal shiny surface is the _____ duplicate of the object.
2. Name the two principles of reflection.
3. Make a sketch of the principles of reflection.
4. When the objects which are to be reflected do not rest on the immediate reflecting surface, what must be done to allow for this?
5. Will reflections show shade and shadows like the objects themselves?
6. If reflections can be constructed in perspective, do you think they can be constructed in pictorial? Explain.
7. Using a simple sketch, illustrate a variety of different shiny surfaces such as water etc. This is a rendering exercise.
8. Can you think of any other method for casting reflections? If so explain.
9. Using simple sketches, illustrate the casting of reflections on a vertical surface.
10. Illustrate the use of geometry and the principle of diagonal lines in casting reflections on vertical surfaces.

CHAPTER 13—PRESENTATION DRAWINGS

1. Describe the importance of presentation drawings.
2. Illustrate what is the concept of sheet organization.
3. Perspective drawings usually exhibit three distinct planes. Name these planes and show a illustration of your choice.
4. Using your own sketching techniques, illustrate what is perspective clues in presentation drawings.
5. How does value and line weight influence a drawing? Illustrate.
6. Show in a series of sketches how overlapping and placement help to give depth clues.
7. What is hierarchy of line value to the presentation drawing?
8. How can a tone of lines help a drawing? Illustrate.
9. What does the word entourage mean with respect to presentation drawing?
10. When rendering the final presentation list several considerations to think about before beginning.

Chapter 14—Diagramming

1. Give a graphic example of point, line, zone, and symbol for diagramming.
2. What is the purpose of diagramming? Explain.
3. Give an example of a bubble diagram. Identify your use.
4. Give an example of a flow diagram.
5. What is a traffic density diagram and how can it be used?
6. Using overlays, illustrate factor analysis.
7. Diagram the steps necessary to place film in your camera.
8. Diagram your habits immediately following your evening meal.
9. Using a typical week of classes as a guide, illustrate the following in a diagram: Amount of time spent on social life.
10. Visit a busy intersection and diagram the circulation of cars and pedestrians.